Hands-On Data Warehousing with Azure Data Factory

ETL techniques to load and transform data from various sources, both on-premises and on cloud

Christian Coté
Michelle Gutzait
Giuseppe Ciaburro

BIRMINGHAM - MUMBAI

Hands-On Data Warehousing with Azure Data Factory

Commissioning Editor: Sunith Shetty
Acquisition Editor: Vinay Argekar
Content Development Editor: Mayur Pawanikar
Technical Editor: Dinesh Pawar
Copy Editors: Vikrant Phadkay, Safis Editing
Project Coordinator: Nidhi Joshi
Proofreader: Safis Editing
Indexer: Rekha Nair
Graphics: Tania Dutta
Production Coordinator: Deepika Naik

First published: May 2018

Production reference: 1300518

Published by Packt Publishing Ltd.
Livery Place
35 Livery Street
Birmingham
B3 2PB, UK.

ISBN 978-1-78913-762-0

www.packtpub.com

`mapt.io`

Mapt is an online digital library that gives you full access to over 5,000 books and videos, as well as industry leading tools to help you plan your personal development and advance your career. For more information, please visit our website.

Why subscribe?

- Spend less time learning and more time coding with practical eBooks and Videos from over 4,000 industry professionals

- Improve your learning with Skill Plans built especially for you

- Get a free eBook or video every month

- Mapt is fully searchable

- Copy and paste, print, and bookmark content

PacktPub.com

Did you know that Packt offers eBook versions of every book published, with PDF and ePub files available? You can upgrade to the eBook version at `www.PacktPub.com` and as a print book customer, you are entitled to a discount on the eBook copy. Get in touch with us at `service@packtpub.com` for more details.

At `www.PacktPub.com`, you can also read a collection of free technical articles, sign up for a range of free newsletters, and receive exclusive discounts and offers on Packt books and eBooks.

Contributors

About the authors

Christian Coté has been in IT for more than 12 years. He is an MS-certified technical specialist in business intelligence (MCTS-BI). For about 10 years, he has been a consultant in ETL/BI projects. His ETL projects have used various ETL tools and plain code with various RDBMSes (such as Oracle and SQL Server). He is currently working on his sixth SSIS implementation in 4 years.

Michelle Gutzait has been in IT for 30 years as a developer, business analyst, and database consultant. She has worked with MS SQL Server for 20 years. Her skills include infrastructure and database design, performance tuning, security, HADR solutions, consolidation, very large databases, replication, T-SQL coding and optimization, SSIS, SSRS, SSAS, admin and infrastructure tools development, cloud services, training developers, DBAs, and more. She has been an Oracle developer, business analyst, and development team lead.

Giuseppe Ciaburro holds a PhD in environmental technical physics and two master's degrees. His research is on machine learning applications in the study of urban sound environments. He works at Built Environment Control Laboratory, Università degli Studi della Campania Luigi Vanvitelli (Italy). He has over 15 years' experience in programming Python, R, and MATLAB, first in the field of combustion, and then in acoustics and noise control. He has several publications to his credit.

About the reviewer

Chirag Nayyar helps organizations to initiate their digital transformation using the public cloud. He has been actively working on cloud platforms since 2013, providing consultancy services to many organizations, ranging from SMBs to Enterprises. He holds a wide range of certifications from all major public cloud platforms. He also runs meetups and is a regular speaker at various cloud events.

He has also reviewed few books published by Packt.

Packt is searching for authors like you

If you're interested in becoming an author for Packt, please visit `authors.packtpub.com` and apply today. We have worked with thousands of developers and tech professionals, just like you, to help them share their insight with the global tech community. You can make a general application, apply for a specific hot topic that we are recruiting an author for, or submit your own idea.

Table of Contents

Preface

Extract, Transform, and Load (ETL) is one of the essential techniques in data processing. Given that data is everywhere, ETL will always be the best way to handle data from different sources.

This book starts with the basic concepts of data warehousing and ETL. You will learn how Azure Data Factory and SSIS can be used to understand the key components of an ETL solution. You will go through different services offered by Azure that can be used by ADF and SSIS, such as Azure Data Lake Analytics, machine learning, and Databrick's Spark, with the help of practical examples. You will explore how to design and implement ETL hybrid solutions using different integration services in a step-by-step approach. Once you get to grips with all this, you will use Power BI to interact with data coming from different sources in order to reveal valuable insights.

By the end of this book, you will not only know how to build your own ETL solutions, but will also be able to address the key challenges that are faced while building them.

Who this book is for

This book is for you if you are a software professional who develops and implements ETL solutions using Microsoft SQL Server or Azure Cloud. It will be an added advantage if you are a software engineer, DW/ETL architect, or ETL developer and know how to create a new ETL implementation or enhance an existing one with Azure Data Factory or SSIS.

What this book covers

Chapter 1, *The Modern Data Warehouse*, teaches us the various storage options available in Microsoft Azure that will help us to set up our Azure factory.

Chapter 2, *Getting Started with Our First Data Factory*, uses the data factory to move data from Azure SQL to Azure storage.

Chapter 3, *SSIS Lift and Shift*, digs further into the various services available in Azure, as well as how we can integrate an existing SSIS solution into the factory.

Chapter 4, *Azure Data Lake*, primarily focuses on the components of the Azure Data Lake and provides a basic implementation of those components.

Chapter 5, *Machine Learning on the Cloud*, recognizes the different machine learning algorithms and the tools that Microsoft Azure Machine Learning Studio provides to handle them.

Chapter 6, *Introduction to Azure Databricks*, shows how Azure Data Factory can trigger Databricks notebook.

Chapter 7, *Reporting on the Modern Data Warehouse*, explains how we can integrate this data into a Power BI report.

To get the most out of this book

- **Azure subscription**. If you don't have a subscription, you can create a free trial account in just a couple of minutes at http://azure.microsoft.com/pricing/free-trial/.
- **Azure storage account**. You use the blob storage as a source data store in this tutorial. If you don't have an Azure storage account, see the how create a storage account at https://docs.microsoft.com/en-us/azure/storage/common/storage-create-storage-account#create-a-storage-account.
- **Azure SQL database**. You'll use an Azure SQL database as a destination data store in this tutorial. If you don't have an Azure SQL database that you can use in the tutorial, see how to create and configure an Azure SQL database to create one at https://docs.microsoft.com/en-us/azure/sql-database/sql-database-get-started.
- **SQL Server 2017 Developer Edition, SQL Server Management Studio or Visual Studio 2015 or 2017**. You can use SQL Server 2017 Developer Editon, SQL Server Management Studio or Visual Studio to create a sample database and to view the result data in the database.

Download the example code files

You can download the example code files for this book from your account at www.packtpub.com. If you purchased this book elsewhere, you can visit www.packtpub.com/support and register to have the files emailed directly to you.

You can download the code files by following these steps:

1. Log in or register at www.packtpub.com.
2. Select the **SUPPORT** tab.
3. Click on **Code Downloads & Errata**.
4. Enter the name of the book in the **Search** box and follow the onscreen instructions.

Once the file is downloaded, please make sure that you unzip or extract the folder using the latest version of:

- WinRAR/7-Zip for Windows
- Zipeg/iZip/UnRarX for Mac
- 7-Zip/PeaZip for Linux

The code bundle for the book is also hosted on GitHub at https://github.com/PacktPublishing/Hands-On-Data-Warehousing-with-Azure-Data-Factory. In case there's an update to the code, it will be updated on the existing GitHub repository.

We also have other code bundles from our rich catalog of books and videos available at https://github.com/PacktPublishing/. Check them out!

Download the color images

We also provide a PDF file that has color images of the screenshots/diagrams used in this book. You can download it here: https://www.packtpub.com/sites/default/files/downloads/HandsOnDataWarehousingwithAzureDataFactory_ColorImages.pdf.

Conventions used

There are a number of text conventions used throughout this book.

CodeInText: Indicates code words in text, database table names, folder names, filenames, file extensions, pathnames, dummy URLs, user input, and Twitter handles. Here is an example: "When we click on it, the adfv2book blade opens."

A block of code is set as follows:

```
SELECT [CustomerID]
      ,[CustomerName]
      ,[CustomerCategoryName]
      ,[PrimaryContact]
      ,[AlternateContact]
      ,[PhoneNumber]
FROM [Website].[Customers]
```

Bold: Indicates a new term, an important word, or words that you see onscreen. For example, words in menus or dialog boxes appear in the text like this. Here is an example: "Select **Databases** and choose **SQL Database**, as shown in the following screenshot."

 Warnings or important notes appear like this.

 Tips and tricks appear like this.

Get in touch

Feedback from our readers is always welcome.

General feedback: Email feedback@packtpub.com and mention the book title in the subject of your message. If you have questions about any aspect of this book, please email us at questions@packtpub.com.

Errata: Although we have taken every care to ensure the accuracy of our content, mistakes do happen. If you have found a mistake in this book, we would be grateful if you would report this to us. Please visit www.packtpub.com/submit-errata, selecting your book, clicking on the Errata Submission Form link, and entering the details.

Piracy: If you come across any illegal copies of our works in any form on the Internet, we would be grateful if you would provide us with the location address or website name. Please contact us at copyright@packtpub.com with a link to the material.

If you are interested in becoming an author: If there is a topic that you have expertise in and you are interested in either writing or contributing to a book, please visit authors.packtpub.com.

Reviews

Please leave a review. Once you have read and used this book, why not leave a review on the site that you purchased it from? Potential readers can then see and use your unbiased opinion to make purchase decisions, we at Packt can understand what you think about our products, and our authors can see your feedback on their book. Thank you!

For more information about Packt, please visit packtpub.com.

The Modern Data Warehouse 1

Azure Data Factory (ADF) is a service that is available in the Microsoft Azure ecosystem. This service allows the orchestration of different data loads and transfers in Azure.

Back in 2014, there were hardly any easy ways to schedule data transfers in Azure. There were a few open source solutions available, such as Apache Falcon and Oozie, but nothing was easily available as a service in Azure. Microsoft introduced ADF in public preview in October 2014, and the service went to general availability in July 2015.

The service allows the following actions:

- Copying data from various sources and destinations
- Calling various computation services, such as HDInsight and Azure data warehouse data transformations
- Orchestrating the preceding activities using time slices and retrying the activities when there is an error

All these activities were available via the Azure portal at first, and in Visual Studio 2013 before **general availability (GA)**.

The need for a data warehouse

A data warehouse is a repository of enterprise data used for reporting and analysis. There have been three waves of data warehouses so far, which we will cover in the upcoming subsections.

Driven by IT

This is the first wave of **business intelligence (BI)**. IT needed to separate operational data and databases from its origin for the following reasons:

- Keep data changes history. Some operational applications purge the data after a while.
- When users wanted to report on the application's data, they were often affecting the performance of the system. IT replicated the operational data to another server to avoid any performance impact on applications.
- Things got more complex when users wanted to do analysis and reports on databases from multiple enterprise's applications. IT had to replicate all the needed systems and make them speak together. This implied that new structures had to be built and new patterns emerged from there: star schemas, **decision support systems (DSS)**, OLAP cubes, and so on.

Self-service BI

Analysts and users always need data warehouses to evolve at a faster pace. This is the second wave of BI and it happened when major BI players such as Microsoft and Click came with tools that enabled users to merge some data with or without data warehouses. In many enterprises, this is used as a temporary source of analytics or proof of concept. On the other hand, not every data could fit at that time in data warehouses. Many ad hoc reports were, and are still, using self-service BI tools. Here is a short list of such tools:

- Microsoft Power Pivot
- Microsoft Power BI
- Click

Cloud-based BI – big data and artificial intelligence

This is the third wave of BI. The cloud capabilities enable enterprises to do more accurate analysis. Big data technologies allows users to base their analysis on much bigger data volumes. This helps them deriving patterns form the data and have technologies that incorporate and modify these patterns. This leads to artificial intelligence or AI.

Technologies used in big data are not that new. They were used by many search engines in the early 21st century such as Yahoo! and Google. They have also been used quite a lot in research faculties in different enterprises. The third wave of BI broaden the usage of these technologies. Vendors such as Microsoft, Amazon, or Google make it available to almost everyone with their cloud offer.]

The modern data warehouse

Microsoft, as well as many other service providers, have listed the concepts of the modern data warehouse as follows:

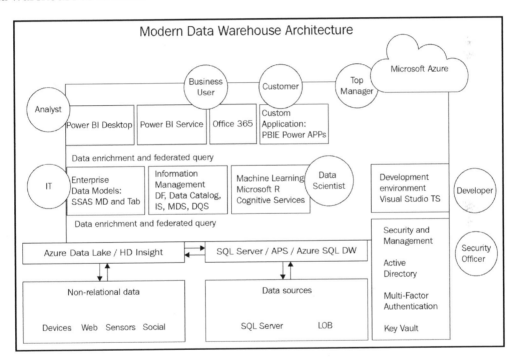

Here are some of the many features a modern data warehouse should have:

- **Integration of relational as well as non-relational sources**: The data warehouse should be able to ingest data that is not easily integrable in the traditional data warehouse, such as big data, non-relational crunched data, and so on.

- **Hybrid deployment**: The data warehouse should be able to extend the data warehouse from on-premises storage to the cloud.
- **Advanced analytics**: The data warehouse should be able to analyze the data from all kinds of datasets using different modern machine learning tools.
- **In-database analytics**: The data warehouse should be able to use Microsoft software that is integrated with some very powerful analytics open tools, such as R and Python, in its database. Also, with PolyBase integration, the data warehouse can integrate more data sources when it's based on SQL Server.

Main components of a data warehouse

This section will discuss the various parts of a data warehouse.

Staging area

In a classic data warehouse, this zone is usually a database and/or a schema in it that used to hold a copy of the data from the source systems. The staging area is necessary because most of the time, data sources are not stored on the same server as the data warehouse. Even if they are on the same server, we prefer a copy of them for the following reasons:

- Preserve data integrity. All data is copied over from a specific point in time. This ensures that we have consistency between tables.
- We might need specific indexes that we could not create in the source system. When we query the data, we're not necessarily making the same links (joins) in the source system. Therefore, we might have to create indexes to increase query performance.
- Querying the source might have an impact on the performance of the source application. Usually, the staging area is used to bring just the changes from the source systems. This prevents processing too much data from the data source.

Not to mention that the data source might be files: CSV, XML, and so on. It's much easier to bring their content in relational tables. From a modern data warehouse perspective, this means storing the files in HDFS and separating them using dates.

In a modern data warehouse, if we're in the cloud only, relational data can still be stored in databases. The only difference might be in the location of the databases. In Azure, we can use Azure SQL tables or Azure data warehouse.

Data warehouse

This is where the data is copied over from the staging area. There are several schools of thought that define the data warehouse:

- **Kimball group data warehouse bus**: Ralph Kimball was a pioneer in data warehousing. He and his colleagues wrote many books and articles on their method. It consists of conformed dimensions that can be used by many business processes. For example, if we have a dimension named DimCustomer, we should link it to all fact tables that store customers. We should not create another dimension that redefines our customers. The following link gives more information on the Kimball group method: `https://www.kimballgroup.com`.
- **Inmon CIF**: Bill Inmon and his colleagues defined the corporate information factory at the end of 1990s. This consisted of modeling the source systems commonly using the third normal form. All the data in the table was dated, which means that any changes in the data sources were inserted in the data warehouse tables. The following link gives more information on CIF: `http://www.inmoncif.com`.
- **Data Vault**: Created by Dan Linsted in the 21st century, this is the latest and more efficient modeling method in data warehousing. It consists of breaking down the source data into many different entities. This gives a lot of flexibility when the data is consumed. We have to reconstruct the data and use the necessary pieces for our analysis. Here is a link that gives more information on Data Vault: `http://learndatavault.com`.

Cubes

In addition to the relational data warehouse, we might have a cube such as SQL Server Analysis Services. Cubes don't replace the relational data warehouses, they extend it. They can also connect to the other part of the warehouse that is not necessarily stored in a relational database. By doing this, they become a semantic layer that can be used by the consumption layer described next.

Consumption layer – BI and analytics

This area is where the data is consumed from the data warehouse and/or the data lake. This book has a chapter dedicated to data lake. In short, the data lake is composed of several areas (data ponds) that classify the data inside of it. The data warehouse is a part of the data lake; it contains the certified data. The data outside the data warehouse in the data lake is most of the time noncertified. It is used to do ad hoc analysis or data discovery.

The BI part can be stored in relational databases, analytic cubes, or models. It can also consist of views on top of the data warehouse when the data is suitable for it.

What is Azure Data Factory

Azure data factories are composed of the following components:

- **Linked services**: Connectors to the various storage and compute services. For example, we can have a pipeline that will use the following artifacts:
    - **HDInsight cluster on demand**: Access to the HDInsight compute service to run a Hive script that uses HDFS external storage
    - **Azure Blob storage/SQL Azure**: As the Hive job runs, this will retrieve the data from Azure and copy it to an SQL Azure database
- **Datasets**: There are layers for the data used in pipelines. A dataset uses a linked service.
- **Pipeline**: The pipeline is the link between all datasets. It contains activities that initiate data movements and transformations. It is the engine of the factory; without pipelines, nothing will move in the factory.

Limitations of ADF V1.0

As good as ADF was, and although a lot of features have been added to it since its GA in 2015, there were a few limitations. At first, we relied on JSON quite a lot to define various ADF abstracts. The number of data stores and compute capabilities were quite limited.

The development experience is very different compared to V2.0. As shown in the following screenshot, we could use the Author and Deploy capability, but it only gave us JSON templates.

As we will see later in this book, the new V2.0 factory has a much better development experience.

When it came to source control, we had to rely on Visual Studio integration. From Visual Studio, we could create or import an existing factory and therefore, use the source control of our choice to version it.

What's new in V2.0?

With V2, ADF has now been overhauled. This section will describe the main novelties of ADF V2.

Integration runtime

This is one of the main features of version 2.0. It represents the compute infrastructure and performs data integration across networks. Here are some enhancements it can provide:

- Data movements between public and private networks either on-premises or using a **virtual private network** (**VPN**). They were known as data management gateways in V1 and Power BI.
  - **Public**: They are used by Azure and other cloud connections. There's a default integration runtime that comes with ADF.
  - **Private**: They are used to connect private computer resources such as SQL Server on-premises to ADF. We need to install a service on one Windows machine in the private network. That machine can connect to the enterprise resources and send the data to ADF via the service installed on it.
- SSIS package execution—managing SSIS packages in Azure. This is one of the main topics of this book. Chapter 3, *SSIS Lift and Shift*, is completely dedicated to this feature.

Linked services

Linked services now have a connectVia property to be able to use the Integration Runtimes that we mentioned in this chapter before. They can now connect to a lot more of data stores than it was possible before.

Datasets

Datasets are the same as they were in V1, but we don't need to define any availability schedules in them now. This means that they have more flexibility in their usage. In conjunction with Linked Services, the datasets have now access to a whole lot of new data stores: sources and destinations.

Pipelines

Pipelines have been modified quite a lot in V2. They don't have any windows of execution, with start times and end times. Pipelines can now be executed using the following technique:

- On demand via .NET, PowerShell, REST API, or Python
- Trigger:
  - **Schedule trigger**: This trigger uses a wall clock kind of schedule, for example, a pipeline can be executed on a weekly basis every Tuesday and Thursday at 10:00 AM
  - **Tumbling window trigger**: This works on a periodic interval, for example, every 15 minutes between two specific dates

Activities

Pipelines now have the following control activities:

- **Execute pipeline**: Calls another pipeline in the same factory.
- **For each activity**: Executes activities in a loop similar to any `for each` loop in structured programming languages.
- **Web activity**: Used to call custom REST endpoints.
- **Lookup activity**: Gets a record from any external data. The output can later be used by subsequent activities.
- **Get metadata activity**: Gets the metadata of activities in ADF.
- **Until activity**: Loops the execution of activity sets until the condition is evaluated to true.
- **If condition activity**: This is like any `if` statement in standard programming languages.
- **Wait activity**: Pauses the pipeline for a time before resuming other activities.

Parameters

Parameters can be used in pipelines. They are read-only values that are passed when the pipeline is executed manually or when they are scheduled to be executed.

Expressions

In V1, functions could be used to filter out dataset queries. In V2, expressions can be used anywhere in JSON-defined factory objects.

Controlling the flow of activities

Calling activities is more flexible in V2 than in the previous one (V1). As stated in the *Pipeline* section, there are many new activities, such as `for each`, `if`, `until`, `lookup`, and so on.

SSIS package deployment in Azure

There is now a new SSI runtime that completely manages clusters of Azure VMs dedicated to running SSIS in the cloud. Packages are deployed in the same manner that they are deployed on-premises when using the Azure SSIS integration runtime. **SQL Server Data Tools (SSDT)** or **SQL Server Management Studio (SSMS)** can be used to deploy SSIS packages.

Spark cluster data store

There are many more data stores available now.

Spark clusters are now available in V2. Since Spark is very performant and now integrates more functionalities, it has become an almost essential player in the big data world. In the previous version of ADF, Spark clusters were available via MapReduce custom activities. In this version, Spark is now a first-class citizen, so there will be no more headaches when it comes to integrating it in our data flow.

Summary

In this chapter, we saw the features of a modern data warehouse. We also saw the new features added in the version 2.0 of ADF.

In the next chapter, we will use the data factory to move data from Azure SQL to Azure storage.

2

Getting Started with Our First Data Factory

OK, enough talk, let's get our hands dirty. In this chapter, we will cover the basics of the data factory and show you what the components discussed in the previous chapter are doing.

Here is what's needed for this chapter, as well as all others in this book:

- An active Azure subscription: if you don't have one, you can use a trial version at `https://azure.microsoft.com/en-in/free/`.
- Once we have an Azure subscription, we will create the following Azure components:
    - A resource group that will group everything we're going to create together
    - An ADF with a copy activity
    - An Azure Blob storage
    - A SQL Azure database

Resource group

To create a resource group, we need to log on to the Azure portal by typing the following URL in a browser: `http://Portal.Azure.com`.

From the resource panel, click on the **+ New** icon and enter `resource group` in the search box, as shown in the following screenshot:

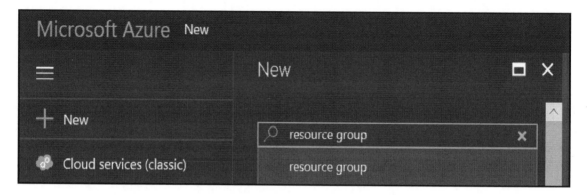

Clicking on the search results opens the **Resource group** blade. We simply need to click **Create** at the bottom of the screen.

As shown in the following screenshot, we'll fill the textboxes with the following properties:

- **Resource group name**: `ADFV2Book`.
- **Subscription**: Should be filled with the active subscription used to create the resource group.
- **Resource group location**: We can choose any location we want. Location is not that important for a resource group but for compliance reasons, we should use a location where all our Azure artifacts will be created.

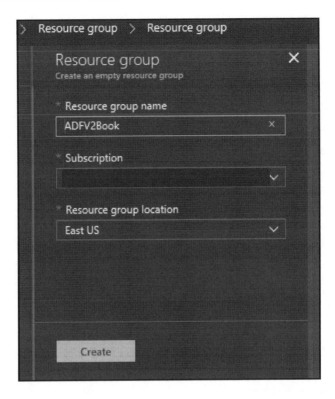

Once we click on **Create** at the bottom of the blade, we get the **Resource group created** notification, as shown in the following screenshot:

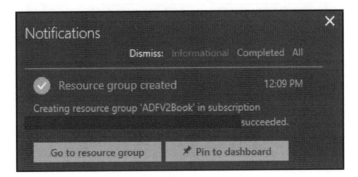

We can pin it to the dashboard if needed. When we click on **Go to resource group**, we get the following blade:

Resource group blade (ADFV2Book)

That's it, our resource group is created! We're now ready to add some Azure artifacts to it. More information on resource groups can be found at https://docs.microsoft.com/en-us/azure/azure-resource-manager/resource-group-overview.

Azure Data Factory

Now, we'll create the factory. The goal of the exercise is to copy data from a SQL Server table and bring it in an Azure Blob storage.

Log in to the Azure portal (http://Portal.Azure.com). In the resource section, click the + **New** icon. Click on **Data + Analytics** and select **Data Factory**, as shown in the following screenshot:

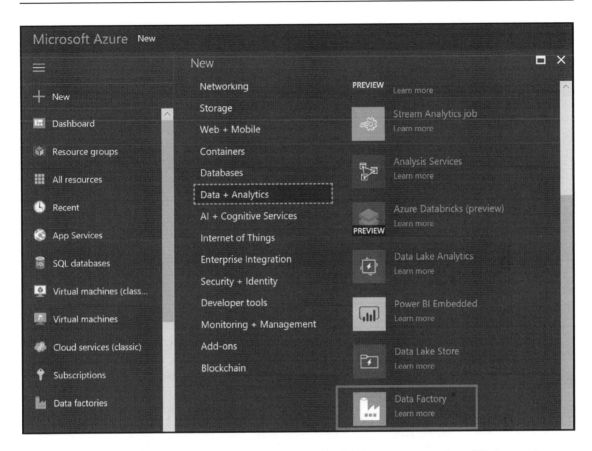

The **New data factory** blade opens. As shown in the following screenshot, fill the textboxes with the following values:

- **Name**: The name of the factory might be later registered as DNS. It should be unique if at all possible. To make it unique, we might use our initials in front of it. There are naming rules for data factories, which can be found at `https://docs.microsoft.com/en-us/azure/data-factory/naming-rules`.
- **Subscription**: Should be filled with the active subscription used to create the data factory.
- **Resource Group**: We're using the resource group created earlier in this chapter.
- **Version**: Since this book talks about V2, we'll use V2 of the data factory. At the time of writing, the version was in preview.

- **Location**: This time, the location is important. We'll choose the one that we used for the resource group; this is also the one that will be closer to our data in Azure to avoid supplemental charges.

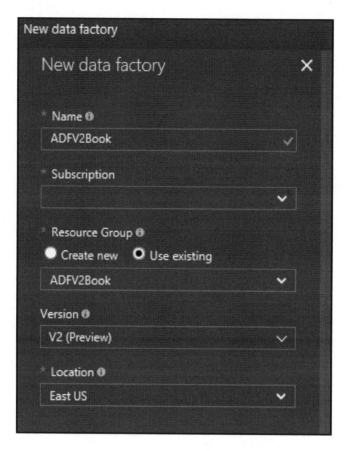

Once we've filled out all properties, we can select **Pin to dashboard** to make our data factory handy. We can click on **Create** to start building the factory:

The factory gets deployed.

Once the factory is created, its blade opens, as shown in the following screenshot:

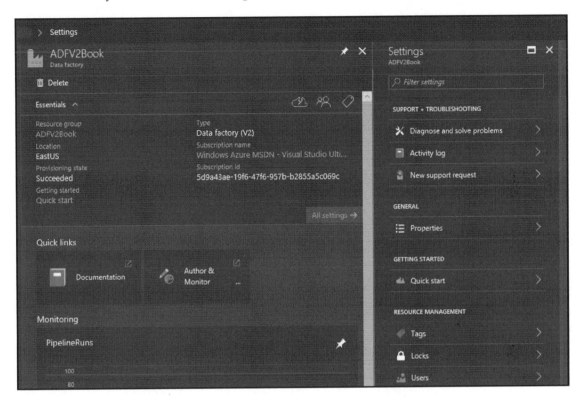

When we click on **Author & Monitor**, the factory's object creation blade opens, as shown in the following screenshot:

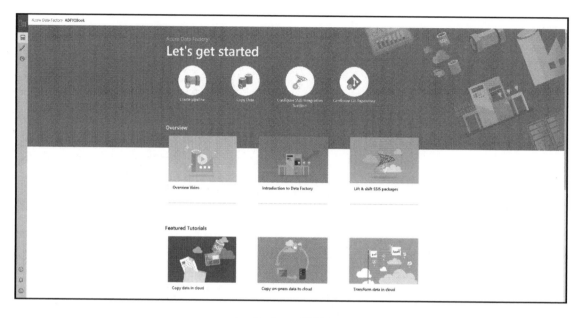

Azure Data Factory (ADFV2Book)

We'll spend a lot of time in the factory's object creation blade. Clicking on the pencil icon, shown in the following screenshot, will bring the editor:

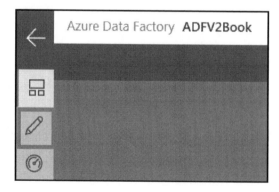

As shown in the following screenshot, the editor is empty. We'll add some objects later:

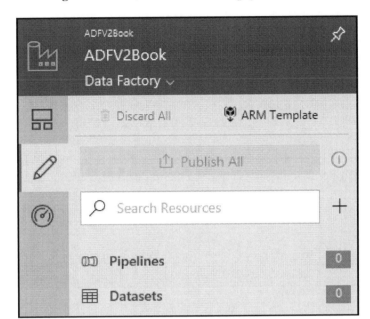

For now, let's talk about the factory pipeline. The pipeline is the heart of the data factory. This is where we define data movements and transformations. There are other types of artifacts related to the pipeline, and we'll talk about them in the next sections: *Linked services*, *Integration runtimes*, *Datasets*, and *Activities*.

Datasets

A dataset is used as an intermediate layer between a pipeline and a data store. When we create a dataset, we're asked to choose what data store we want to connect to, a linked service. A dataset also contains a schema, which is the tabular representation of our data. We'll create a dataset later in this chapter and we'll review these concepts.

Linked services

Linked services are like an SSIS connection manager. There are as many linked services as data sources used in the pipeline. For example, to interact with a database, the dataset will ask us to enter the connection details of the database.

Integration runtimes

Integration runtimes are used by ADF to provide infrastructure for our data integration for sources that are in different networks. There are three types of integration runtime:

- **Azure integration runtime**: This is used for activities between cloud objects in Azure virtual networks.
- **Self-hosted integration runtime**: This is used for activities between cloud and private or on-premises networks, for example, copying data between an on-premises data warehouse and an Azure Blob storage.
- **Azure-SSIS integration runtime**: This is used to execute SSIS packages in Azure. We'll have a dedicated chapter for this integration runtime.

Activities

Once we have a connection and a schema of the data we want to play with, we need an activity to move it from one point to another—copy activity—or when the data has to be transformed, a compute activity.

We'll see later in this chapter how to configure and execute an activity in our pipeline.

Monitoring the data factory pipeline runs

Once we start using a pipeline in our factory, we want to know how and when it runs. This is the monitoring part of our data factory. As shown in the following screenshot, clicking on the gauge icon on the left, under the pencil, will bring up the **Pipeline Runs** monitor:

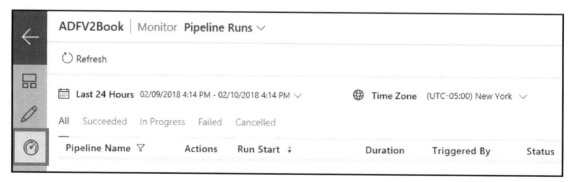

Since we haven't created or executed any pipelines in our factory yet, the monitoring part of it is empty.

Azure Blob storage

At the heart of the Azure ecosystem is the blob storage service. This service, as its name indicates, provides file storage. There are different types of blobs, as not all of them are created equally. The next few sections will describe the different blobs and their usage.

Blob containers

Blob containers are the first level of blob storage. All blobs need a container as root access. It's like a folder in a standard operating system.

Types of blobs

There are several types of blobs for different usage. The next sections briefly describe the various blob types. For more information, please see the following link:
`https://docs.microsoft.com/en-us/azure/storage/`.

Block blobs

Block blobs are used by most Azure data transfers. They can store application files (CSV, ZIP, and so on), tables used by NoSQL applications, and queues used by streaming services such as Azure **ML** (short for **Azure Machine Learning**). Throughout the examples in this book, we'll use block blobs as storage for some of our data transfers.

Page blobs

Page blobs are used for large file storage. Azure **Virtual Machines (VMs)** use this type of blob to store their disk image.

Replication of storage

Replication of storage represents how the blobs are replicated to ensure the safety of their contents in case of hardware failure. When we create a blob, one of the options we have to select is the replication type:

- **LRS (short for Local Redundant Storage)**: This storage replicates each blob three times in the same data center. It is designed to give us 99.999999999% (eleven 9s) in terms of durability of our objects. This is the least expensive option but offers less durability than other options.

- **ZRS (short for Zone Redundant Storage)**: This storage replicates each blob in different zones. It is designed to give us 99.9999999999% (twelve 9s) in terms of durability of our objects. It's used to avoid downtime for applications that use them.

- **GRS (short for Geo-Redundant Storage)**: This storage replicates each blob across Azure regions. Once a blob is written in the primary region, it is replicated asynchronously in a region that might be hundreds of kilometers away. This storage manages to give us 9.99999999999999% (sixteen 9s) in terms of durability. It allows making our data available even if a disaster happens in the primary region.

- **RA-GRS (short for Read-Access Geo-Redundant Storage)**: Similar to GRS, the difference is that the secondary region is made available in read-only mode. This makes applications that use it much more scalable in term of read access performance.

All these options are available when we create a blob storage account. The more durability we have, the more it will cost. The following URL gives an overview of the costs associated with these storage options: `https://azure.microsoft.com/en-us/pricing/details/storage/blobs/`.

Creating an Azure Blob storage account

This section will describe step by step how to create an Azure Blob storage account:

1. Log in the Azure portal and go to **New | Data + Storage | Storage Account**. You should get the **Storage account - blob, file, table, queue** window, as shown in the following screenshot:

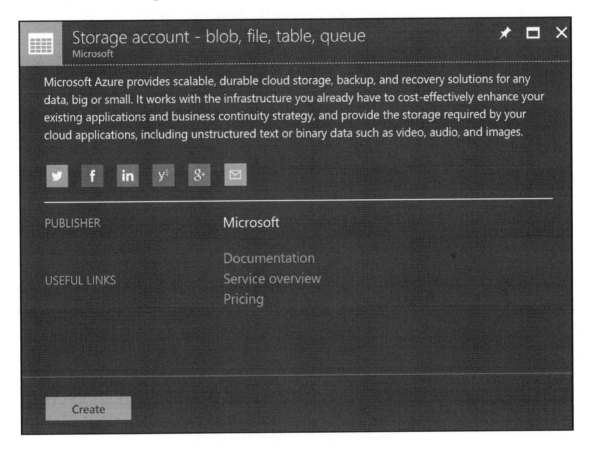

2. Clicking **Create** will bring up **Create storage account**, as shown in the following screenshot:

Fill in the properties as follows:

- **Name:** `adfv2book`.
- **Deployment model: Resource manager.**
- **Account kind: StorageV2 (general purpose v2).**
- **Performance: Standard.**
- **Replication: Locally-redundant storage (LRS).**
- **Access tier (default): Hot.** This means that the data will be accessed frequently.
- **Secure transfer required: Disabled.** Whether the blob will be accessed using HTTP or HTTPS.
- **Subscription:** The current subscription in use when you create the storage account.
- **Resource group:** `ADFV2CookBook`.
- **Location:** We used **East US.** Choose the location used when the resource group was created.
- **Virtual networks:** No VPN will be used for now. Leave this option on **Disabled.**
- **Pin to dashboard:** Check this box if you want the storage to appear on the Azure dashboard.

3. Click on **Create** to create the new Azure storage account.

4. Once the blob has been created and is visible on the dashboard, click on it. You should get something similar to the following screenshot:

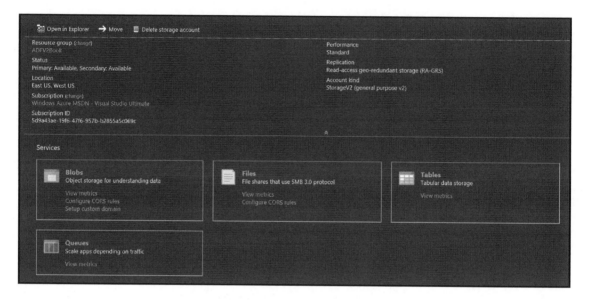

Azure Blob storage account window

5. We'll now click on the **Open in Explorer** icon in the top left; we get a message like the one in the following screenshot:

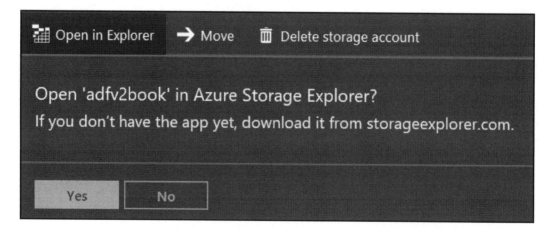

If the application is not installed, we'll be directed to the application download page:

6. We download and install the application. Once installed, we're asked to log in to our Azure account.

7. Once logged in, we choose our Azure subscription, as shown in the following screenshot:

We can now see the content of our Azure Blob storage. For now, it's empty; we'll fill it out later in the exercises in this book:

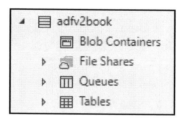

SQL Azure database

We'll now set up a database that will be used by our factory to copy data from. The Wide World Importers sample database is available at: `https://github.com/Microsoft/sql-server-samples/releases/tag/wide-world-importers-v1.0`.

A BACPAC is a file that contains database structures and data, similar to a database backup. The difference is that a BACPAC is a snapshot of a database at a specific time. A database backup is much more than that: the database can be restored up to the last few seconds. Also, a database backup can be incremental—that is, contain data and structures since the last backup. A BACPAC always contains all data.

The version we're using is the standard one, as shown in the following screenshot:

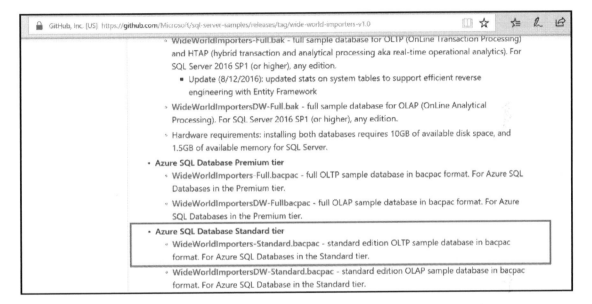

We'll now upload the BACPAC to the storage that we created in the previous section:

1. Open **Microsoft Azure Storage Explorer** and right-click on the `adfv2book` storage account to create a container called `database-bacpac`, as shown in the following screenshot:

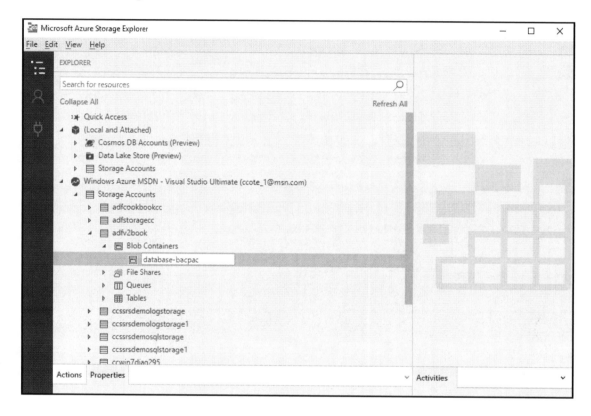

2. Now, click **Upload files** in the rightmost section of the application. Upload the file previously downloaded:

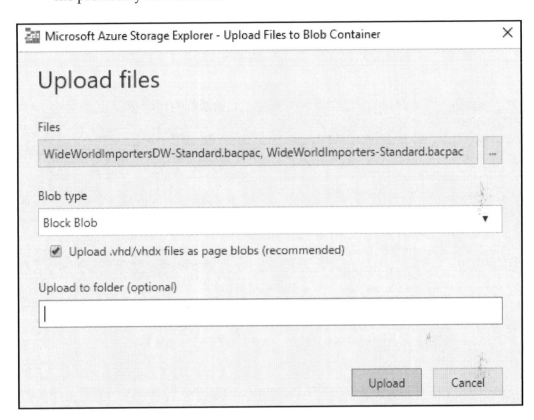

Creating the Azure SQL Server

1. Log in to the Azure portal at https://Portal.Azure.com.
2. In the resources tab, click the **+ New** icon.
3. Select **Databases** and choose **SQL Database**, as shown in the following screenshot:

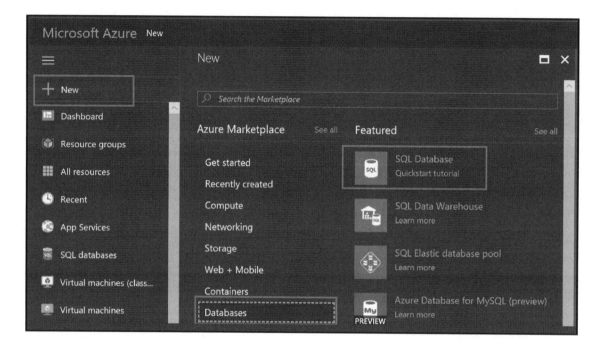

The **SQL Database** blade appears as follows:

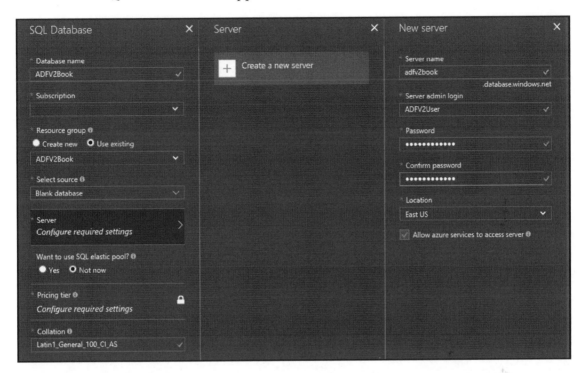

Assign the following properties, shown in the preceding screenshot:

- **Database name**: ADFV2Book.
- **Subscription**: Should already be populated with the active subscription.
- **Resource group**: ADFV2Book.
- **Select source**: **Blank database**, we'll attach one later using the BACPAC downloaded in a previous step.
- **Server**: Click on **Create a new server**:
    - **Server name**: adfv2book
    - **Server admin login**: ADFV2User
    - **Password**: pwADFBook!

Click on **Select** at the bottom of the blade.

Select **Pin to dashboard** and click on **Create** at the bottom of the **SQL Database** blade.

We are directed to the dashboard and see that the database is deploying, as shown in the following screenshot:

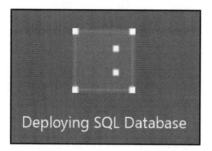

Once the database in created, we need to access it. There is a tool available, the query editor. On the left side of the blade, there's a link to it. Clicking on it brings up the login blade. When we enter the password for `ADFV2User`, we get the query editor, as shown in the following screenshot:

Our database server and our database are created; we are now ready to attach a sample database to it.

Attaching the BACPAC to our database

We previously copied a BACPAC to our Azure storage. Now, we'll import it into the newly created server. From the Azure portal, go to the Azure **SQL servers** blade; we now see our newly created SQL Server, as shown in the following screenshot:

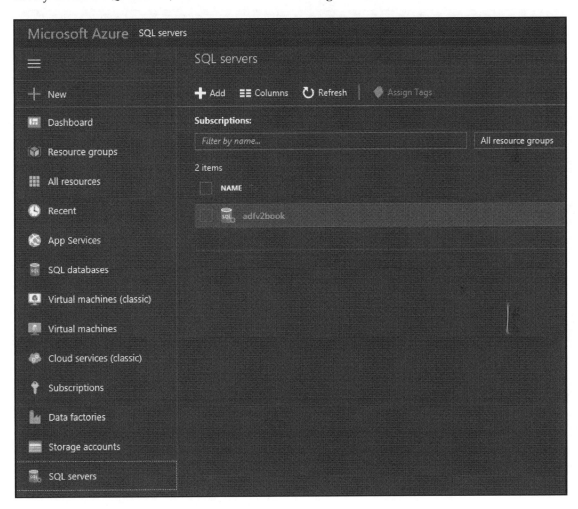

When we click on it, the `adfv2book` blade opens. In the top-middle of it, we click on the **Import database** icon, as shown in the following screenshot:

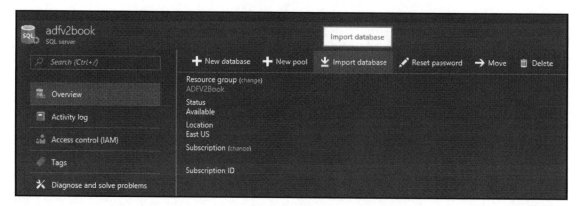

This brings us to the import blade. Select the `adfv2book` storage account and navigate to the **database-bacpac** blob. Select **WideWorldImporters-Standard.bacpac** and click **Select**.

Now, select the **Pin to dashboard** option and click on **Select** to restore the BACPAC, as shown in the following screenshot:

Now, back to the **SQL servers** blade, we'll click on the **Firewall / Virtual Networks** icon at the left to open the server firewall blade. As show in the following screenshot, we click on **Add client IP** to whitelist our network and therefore be able to query the server's databases. Once our IP is added, we click **Save** to keep it:

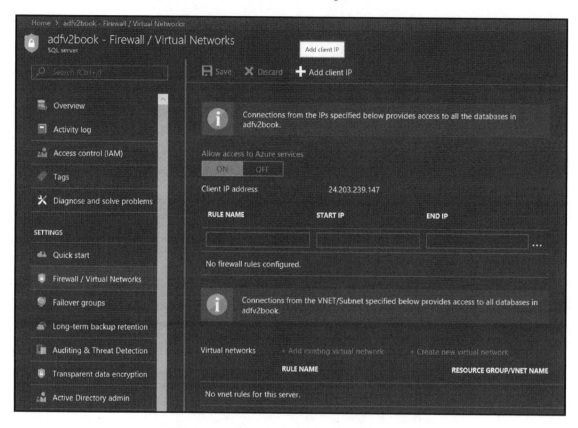

To query the database easily, we'll use SSMS. This program is available freely from Microsoft at the following URL:

```
https://docs.microsoft.com/en-us/sql/ssms/download-sql-server-management-studio
-ssms.
```

Choose the latest version (17.5 at time of writing), download, and install it. Once installed, start SSMS and connect to the server in Azure. Once done, we expand the databases node and we can query tables as shown in the following screenshot:

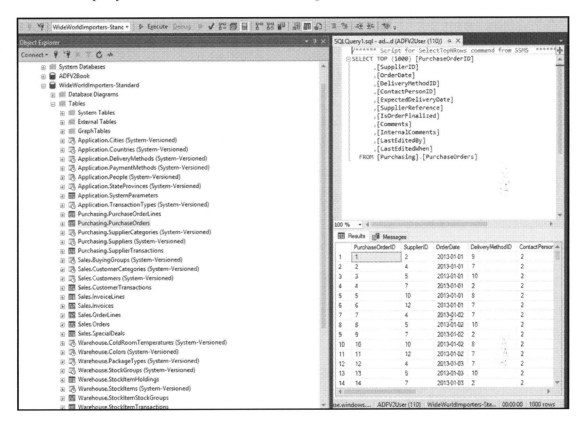

Object explorer with query editor

Copying data using our data factory

OK, we're now ready to implement our first pipeline, that is, copy data from our SQL Server to our Azure storage account. We'll go back to the Azure portal and open our data factory. Once in there, we'll navigate to its details by clicking on **Author & Monitor**. As shown in the following screenshot, we'll select **Copy Data** from the **Let's get started** section:

The **Copy Data** wizard appears. As shown in the following screenshot, we'll fill in the **Properties** section and click **Next**:

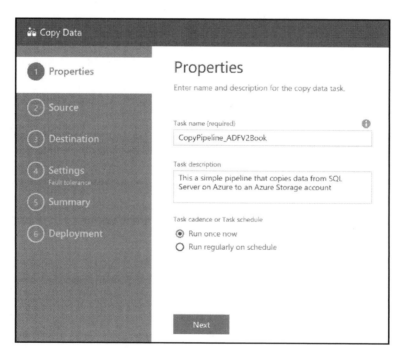

The details to be filled in are as follows:

- **Task name**: `CopyPipeline_ADFV2Book`
- **Task description**: Enter a description, as shown in the preceding screenshot
- **Task cadence or Task schedule**: Select **Run once now**

We're now directed to the **Source** blade. Select **Azure SQL Database** as our source, the one we created earlier in this chapter. Click **Next**:

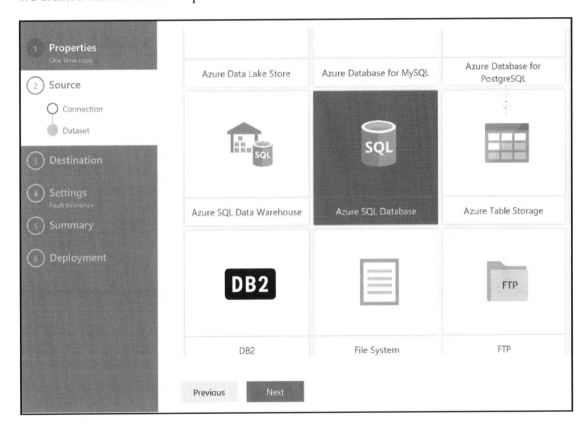

Fill in the **Connection** properties as shown in the following list and click **Next** once done:

- **Connection name**: `Source_SQLAzure_wwimporters`
- **Network environment: Public network in Azure Environment**
- **Server/database selection method: From Azure subscriptions**
- **Azure subscription**: The current subscription used to create the factory

- **Server name**: ADFV2Book; you should use another name since server names are unique in Azure
- **Database name**: WideWorldImporters-Standard
- **Authentication**: **SQL Authentication**

In the table selection blade, we'll click on **USE QUERY** and we'll enter the following query:

```
SELECT [CustomerID]
      ,[CustomerName]
      ,[CustomerCategoryName]
      ,[PrimaryContact]
      ,[AlternateContact]
      ,[PhoneNumber]
      ,[FaxNumber]
      ,[BuyingGroupName]
      ,[WebsiteURL]
      ,[DeliveryMethod]
      ,[CityName]
  FROM [Website].[Customers]
```

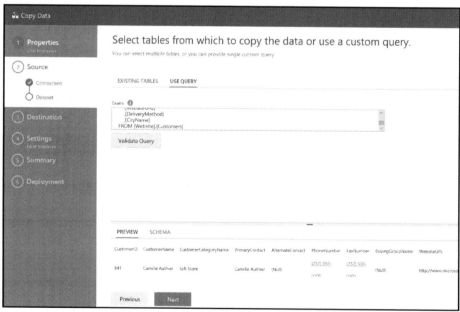

Table selection blade

You should get something similar to that shown in the following screenshot. Click **Next**:

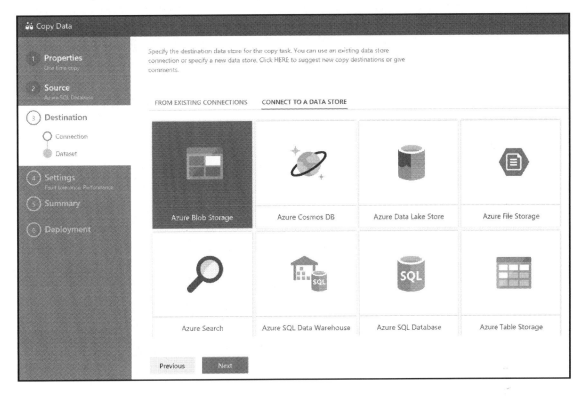

Destination data store for copy task

In the **Destination** selection blade, we'll choose **Azure Blob Storage** and click **Next**, as shown in the following screenshot.

In the **Dataset** blade, fill in the properties as shown in the following screenshot the following list:

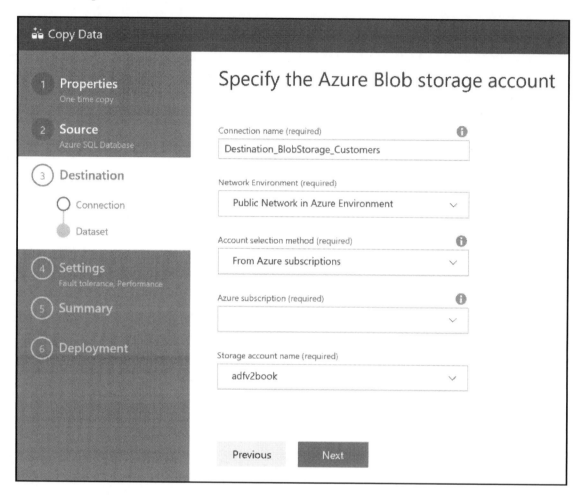

- **Connection name:** `Destination_BlobStorage_Customers`
- **Network Environment: Public Network in Azure Environment**
- **Account selection method: From Azure subscriptions**
- **Azure subscription:** The current subscription used to create the factory
- **Storage account name:** Name of the storage account selected

Clicking **Next** will bring us to the destination file or folder choice. We'll use `website-customer` as the filename.

Clicking **Next** will bring us to the **File format settings** blade. Fill out the properties, as shown in the following screenshot and described later:

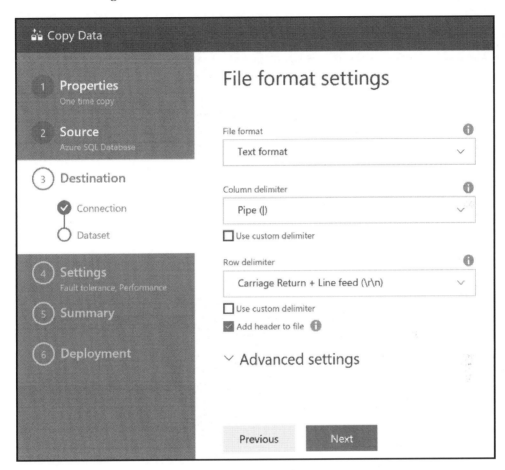

- **File format**: We have several choices between text, Avro, JSON, ORC, and Parquet format; we'll use the **Text format**.
- **Column delimiter**: We'll use the **Pipe(|)** delimiter. We could also use a custom delimiter if we check the Use custom delimiter checkbox.
- **Row delimiter**: We'll use the default, **Carriage return + Line feed (\r\n)**. Again, we could use a custom delimiter here. We'll check the **Add header to file** option.

Clicking **Next** will bring up the **Settings** blade. There, we can adjust fault tolerance, performance, and parallel settings. We'll keep the default values, as shown in the following screenshot:

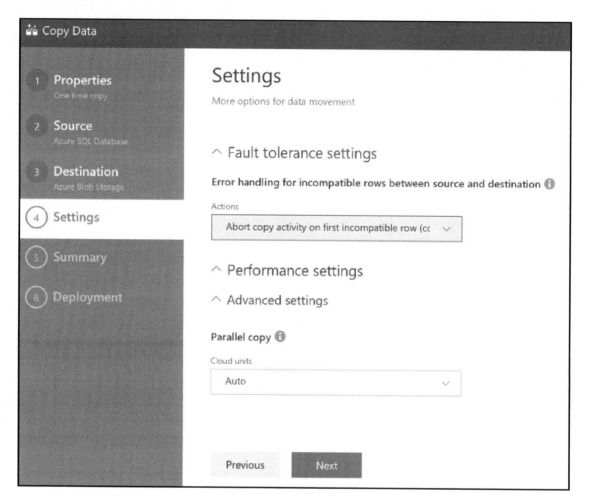

Clicking **Next** will direct us to the **Summary** blade. As shown in the following screenshot, we can see a summary of our pipeline:

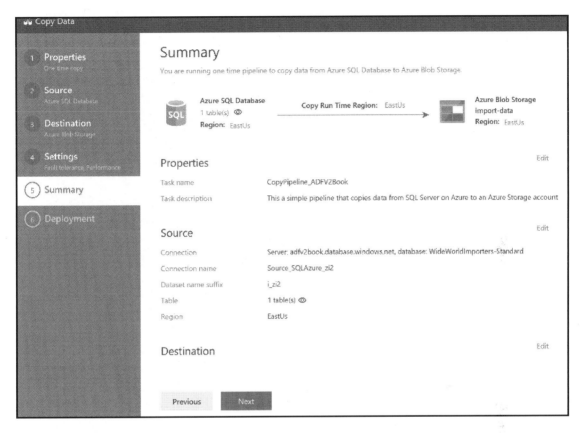

Summary blade (summary of pipelines)

Clicking **Next** will deploy the factory and it'll run the pipeline. Once the pipeline is triggered, we can click on the Monitoring icon at the left of the factory blade to go into the pipeline's run details, as shown in the following screenshot:

Factory blade (ADFV2Book)

Once the pipeline has run successfully, we'll return to our blob storage account. We click on **Blobs** in the blob service, as shown in the following screenshot:

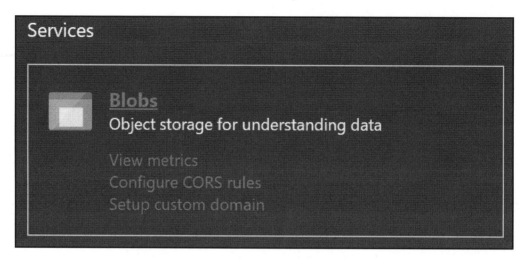

This will open the **Blob service** pane. As shown in the following screenshot, we can see two containers. We'll select the `import-data` container to see its content. The `website-customer` blob appears on the right pane of the blade:

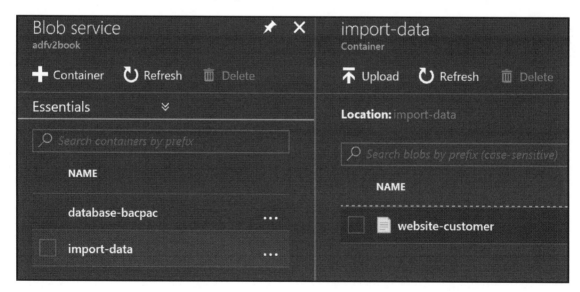

When we right-click on the file, a contextual menu appears. We'll select **Edit**, as shown in the following screenshot:

The edit blade opens for our `website-customer` blade, as shown in the following screenshot:

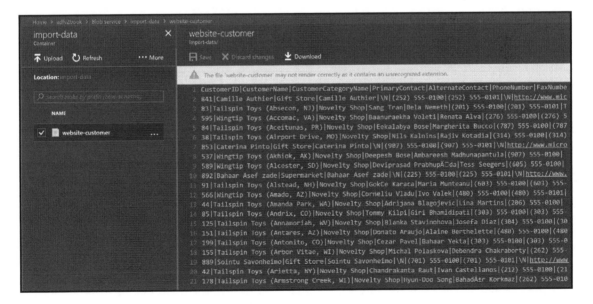

Summary

In this chapter, we created our factory with a pipeline that copies data from an Azure SQL database to an Azure storage account. The following chapters will dig more into the various services available in Azure as well as how we can integrate an existing SSIS solution into the factory.

3

SSIS Lift and Shift

In this chapter, we will talk about the different services that can be used by ADF and SSIS in Azure. SSIS packages can now be integrated with ADF, and can be scheduled/orchestrated using ADF V2. The SSIS package execution capability makes all fine-grained transformation capabilities and SSIS connectors available from within ADF.

In this chapter, we will cover:

- SSIS in ADF
- Leveraging our package in ADF V2

SSIS in ADF

SQL Server Integration Services (SSIS) has been the Microsoft ETL predilection tool for more than a decade. A lot of enterprises have used SSIS to load their on-premises data warehouses since its inception in SQL Server 2005.

In the last couple of years, IT departments have had to deal with different kinds of data and specific toolsets to process them. SSIS has successfully been able to access cloud data from on-premises ETL servers since 2015 with the Azure Feature Pack (`https://docs.microsoft.com/en-us/sql/integration-services/azure-feature-pack-for-integration-services-ssis?view=sql-server-2017`). However, issues occur when most of the ETL is in the cloud and SSIS is in a small part of the chain. And, up until now, it was very complex to use ADF V1 as the orchestrator in the cloud, with some SSIS package calls in the pipeline.

The following sections will describe how SSIS on-premises can be successfully leveraged to interact with cloud data in ADF V2.

Sample setup

The first thing that must be done is setting up an SSIS solution. For simplicity, we'll use Microsoft wide world importers, just like we did in the previous chapter. The samples can be found at `https://github.com/Microsoft/sql-server-samples/releases/tag/wide-world-importers-v1.0`.

From the list, we'll download the databases and SSIS solution:

- `Daily.ETL.ispac`: This is the SSIS solution that takes data from `WideWorldImporters` to the `WideWorldImportersDW` database
- `WideWorldImporters-Full.bacpac`: This is the transactional database that is used as a source for the data warehouse
- `WideWorldImportersDW-Full.bacpac`: This is the sample data warehouse database that we'll use in this chapter, and beyond

Sample databases

The first step is to set up sample databases. For this to happen, we need to install **SQL Server Management Studio (SSMS)**. This program is freely available from Microsoft at `https://docs.microsoft.com/en-us/sql/ssms/download-sql-server-management-studio-ssms`.

Starting SSMS, connect to your server and right-click on the `Databases` folder in the **Object Explorer**. Select **Import Data-tier Application...** from the contextual menu, as shown in the following screenshot:

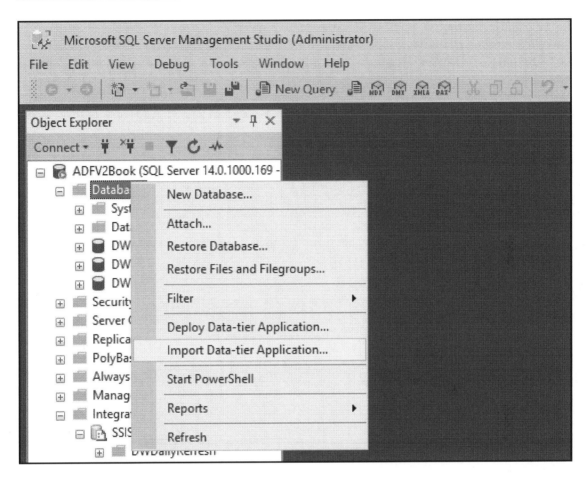

The **Import Data-tier Application** wizard will open. Click on **Next**.

In the **Import Settings** step, make sure that the option **Import from local disk** is selected, and click **Browse...**. From the **Open** window that appears, navigate to the location where you previously downloaded the .bacpac files, and click **Open**, as shown in the following screenshot:

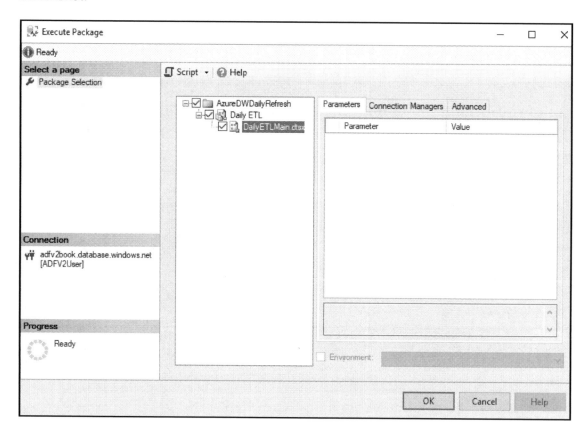

Back on the **Import Settings** screen, click on **Next**.

Next up is the **Database Settings** step. Make sure that the entry in the **New database name** textbox is WideWorldImporters, and click **Next**.

The **Summary** then displays, as shown in the following screenshot. Click on **Finish** to start the BACPAC import process:

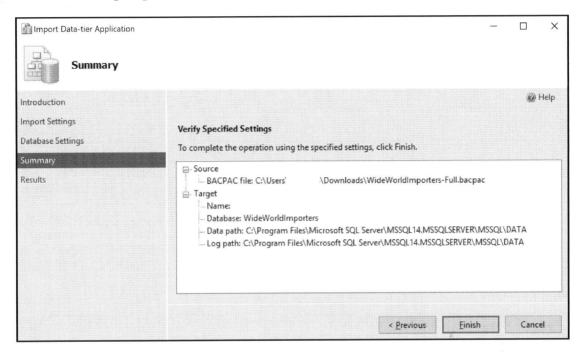

The database is created, as well as all of the objects in it, as shown in the following screenshot. This process may take several minutes. Click **Close** to terminate the process:

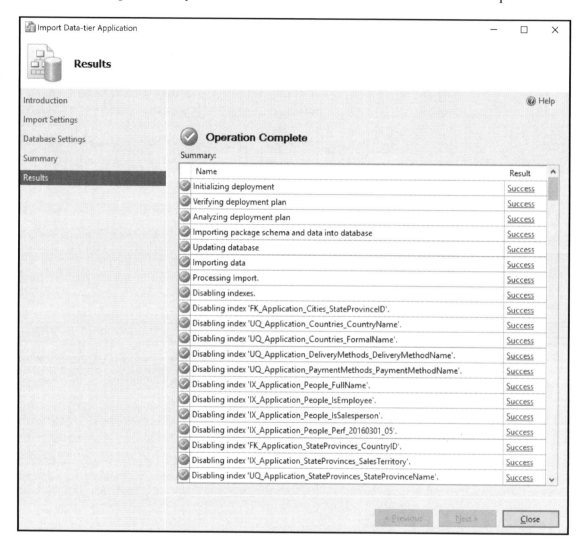

Repeat the same process for the other BACPAC: `WideWorldImportersDW-Full.bacpac`. Make sure that you specify `WideWorldImportersDW` as the database name.

SSIS components

SSIS setup usually requires an existing installation of SQL Server, with the Integration Services feature selected. With ADF V2, this step is less mandatory, since we're going to deploy the packages in an Azure database.

That being said, it's always better to test your SSIS solution on-premises before deploying it in Azure. The next section will describe how to set up the sample SSIS solution that was downloaded earlier in this chapter.

Integration services catalog setup

This step is necessary for brand new, unused SQL Server installations, where we want to deploy SSIS packages. When logged in to the server with SSMS, we simply right-click on the `Integration Services Catalogs` folder and choose **Create Catalog...**

The **Create Catalog** window appears. We fill in the properties and click on **OK** to create the integration services catalog:

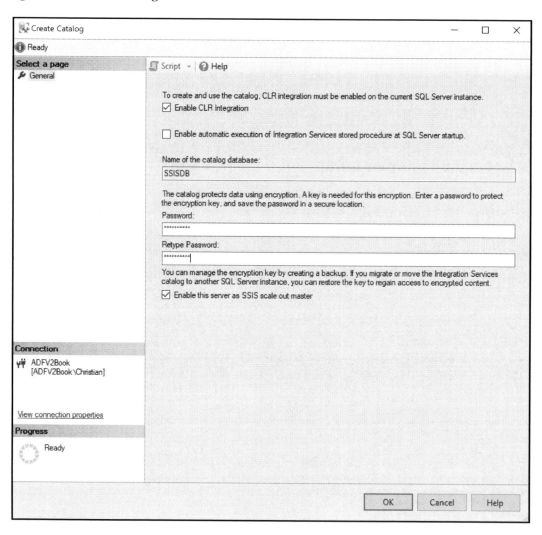

Next, we'll create a folder for our project. In the **Object Explorer**, expand the `Integration Services Catalogs` node, right-click on `SSISDB`, and choose **Create Folder...** from the contextual menu that appears:

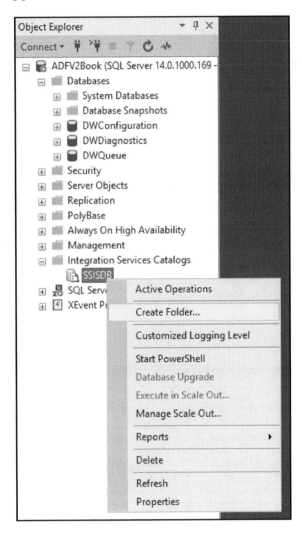

The **Create Folder** window appears. Set the properties to something similar to those shown in the following screenshot, and click on **OK**:

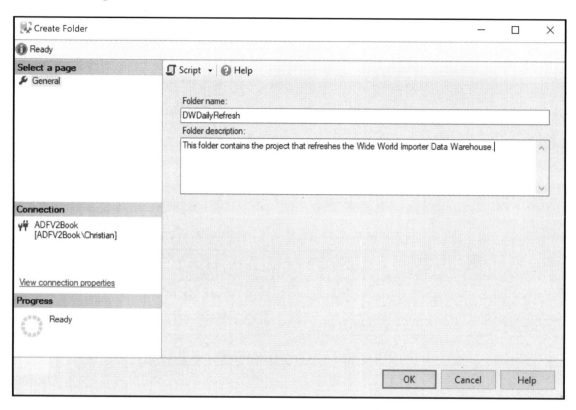

We're now ready to open the solution in Visual Studio. From there, we'll deploy it to our newly created on-premises `Integration Services Catalogs` folder.

Sample solution in Visual Studio

For this section, we'll need an existing installation of Visual Studio 2015 or 2017 and **SQL Server Data Tools (SSDT)** installed. Visual Studio is available at `https://docs.microsoft.com/en-us/sql/ssdt/download-sql-server-data-tools-ssdt?view=sql-server-2017`.

Once SSDT is opened, click on **FILE | New | Project...**:

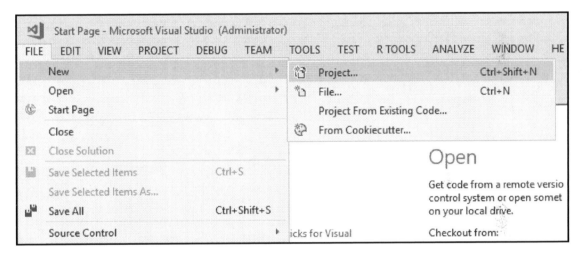

Visual Studio (SSDT)

The **New Project** window appears. Select **Integration Services Import Project Wizard**, type
WWImportersDaily in the textbox beside **Name**, and click on **OK**:

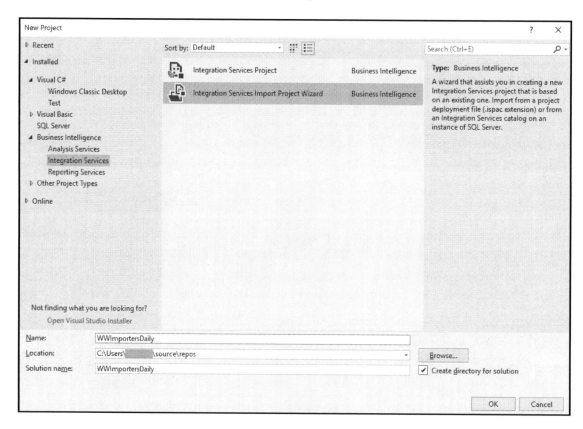

The **Integration Services Import Project Wizard** window opens, as shown in the following screenshot. Click on **Next** to proceed to the next step:

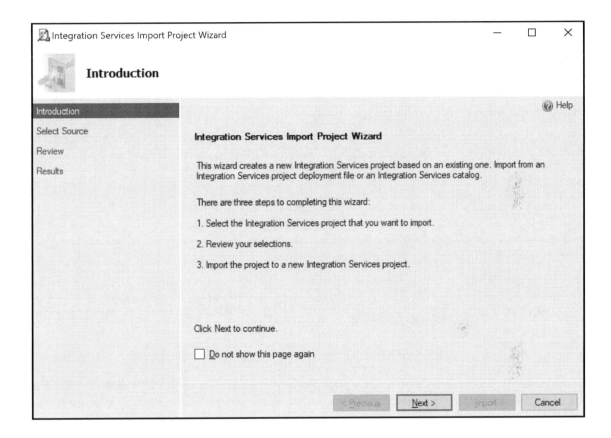

In the **Select Source** window, select the **Project deployment file** radio button, and click on **Browse....** The **Open** file window appears. Navigate to the folder where the SSIS sample file, .ispac, has been downloaded, and click on **Open**:

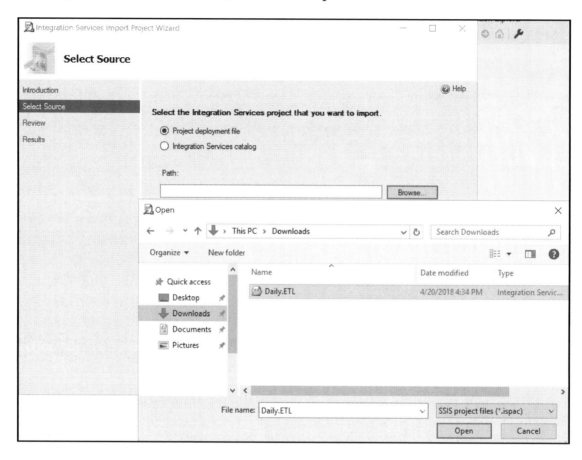

Once back on the wizard, click **Next** to proceed to the next step.

In the **Review** window, click the **Import** button.

Once the project has been imported, you can see it in the **Solution Explorer**:

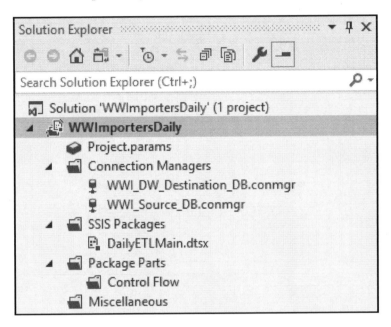

You will have to modify the two connection managers if your server is not the default instance on your server. To do so, double-click on each connection manager, WWI_DW_Destination_DW.conmgr and WWI_Source_DB.conmgr, and change their server properties.

If the connections are online, we can run the package and see if everything is working fine.

Deploying the project on-premises

We're now ready to deploy and test our project on our local server:

1. From the **Solution Explorer**, right-click on the project, WWImportersDaily, and choose **Deploy**. The **Integration Services Deployment Wizard** appears, as shown in the following screenshot.

2. Click **Next** to proceed to the next step:

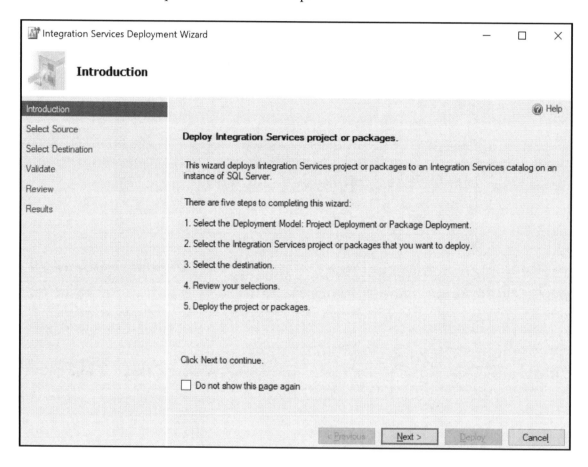

3. Connect to your SQL Server, where the integration services catalog was created before, and click **Browse....** The **Browse for Folder or Project** window will open.

4. Expand SSISDB, and select the DWDailyRefresh folder. We created that folder earlier.

5. Click **OK** to close that window:

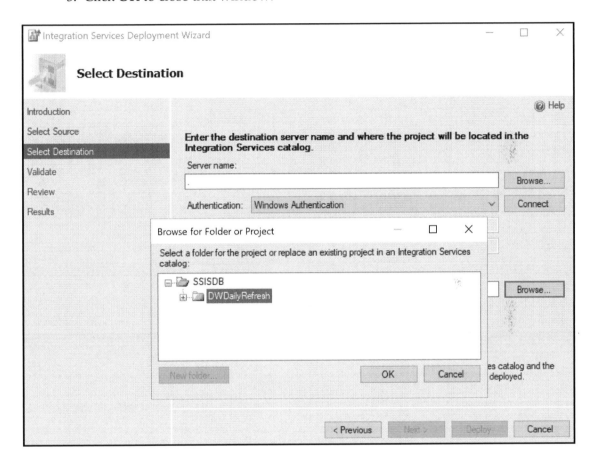

6. Back on the **Select Destination** window, click **Next**.
7. The next step is to validate. On-premises deployments don't use it, however.
8. Click **Next** to proceed to the **Review** window, as shown in the following screenshot. Here, we review whether we have selected the right .ispac file and confirm that we are going to deploy it to the right folder in SSIS, as shown in the following screenshot.
9. Once done, we click on **Deploy** to start the deployment of the .ispac file:

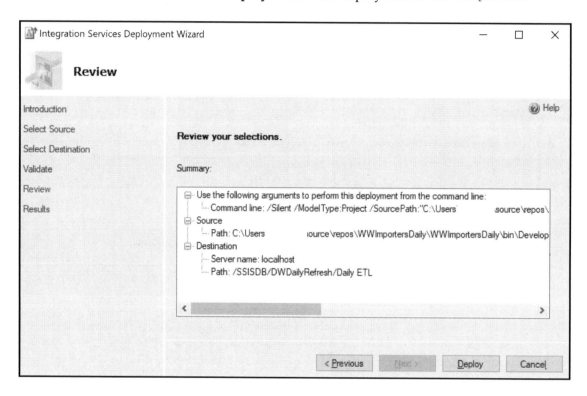

10. The last step, **Results**, shows the progress of our deployment. If everything is successful (as it should be), click the **Close** button:

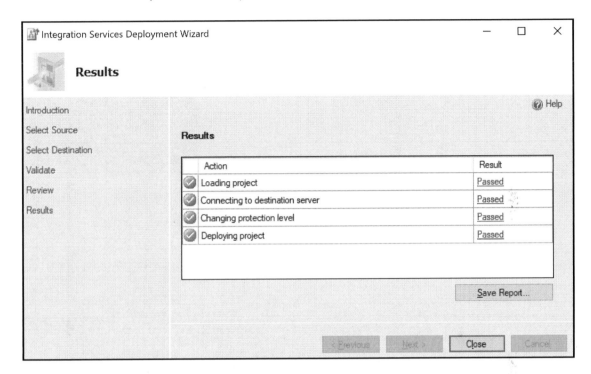

We're now done with the deployment.

11. The next step is to execute the package via the catalog. We'll switch to SQL Server Management Studio for that.

12. In the object explorer, expand the Integration Services Catalogs, and navigate through the DailyETLMain.dtsx package.

13. Right-click on it and select **Execute...** from the contextual menu that appears:

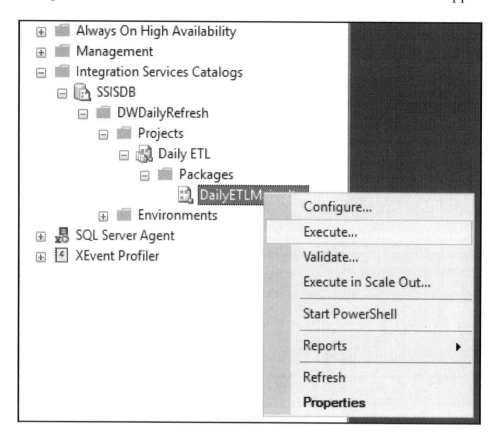

The execution window will appear.

14. Go to the **Connection Managers** tab, as shown in the following screenshot.

15. Check the **Connection String** property for both connectors, and adjust them if necessary.

16. When everything is okay, click on **OK** to start the package execution:

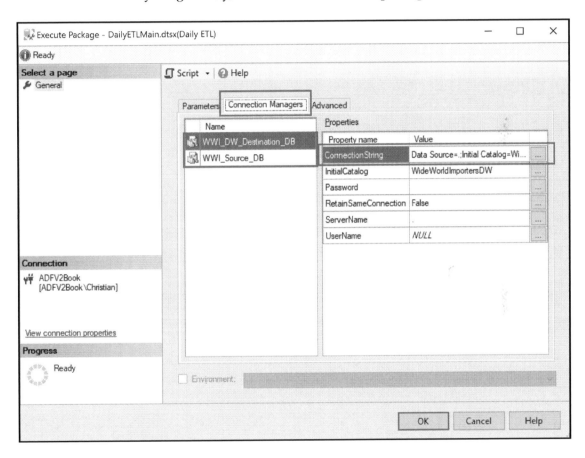

17. Click **Yes** to see the report.

Once the report has opened, we might notice that the package is still running, but when we refresh it, we will see the result, as the package executed with success:

Operation ID	6
Package	DWDailyRefresh\Daily ETL\DailyETLMain.dtsx
Environment	-
Status	Succeeded
Machine	

Execution Overview

Filter: Result: All; (3 more)

Result	Duration (sec)	Package Name	Task Name	Execution Path
Succeeded	7.859	DailyETLMain.dtsx	DailyETLMain	\DailyETLMain
Succeeded	0.016	DailyETLMain.dtsx	Calculate ETL Cutoff Time backup	\DailyETLMain\Calculate ETL Cutoff Time backup
Succeeded	0.109	DailyETLMain.dtsx	Ensure Date Dimension	\DailyETLMain\Ensure Date

Leveraging our package in ADF V2

So far, we haven't done anything new, in the sense that everything we did was on-premises. This part of the book will focus on cloud leveraging of SSIS packages.

Before ADF V2, the only way to achieve orchestration with SSIS was to schedule our SSIS load on an on-premises (or an Azure) virtual machine, and then schedule an ADF V1.0 pipeline every n amount of minutes. If the data was not available at a specific time, the next ADF run would take it. Or, we had to tell ADF to wait for it before processing the rest of its pipeline.

Also, with the advent of SSIS 2017, the scaling out of package execution had to be done on-premises. There are a couple of issues with it:

- Who is responsible for the data warehouse data different usage? The developers that create and maintain the packages are not necessarily aware of the cloud implications of their processes. The data might be used in systems other than the ones they had in their specifications, when they first developed the SSIS packages. The SSIS packages might be running in an acceptable, timely fashion on-premises, but the pace might need to be faster for further analytical usage in the cloud.
- The packages were developed with a paradigm that can evolve, and the development team does not necessarily want to redevelop everything from scratch in the cloud.

For these reasons, and probably more, the ADF team integrated SSIS in version 2 of the product.

Integration runtimes

We discussed integration runtimes briefly in the first chapter of this book. We'll now expand on them in this section.

Azure integration runtime

This integration runtime is used by ADF to connect to cloud computing services, like HDInsight, and Azure data stores, like Blob storage. Every factory has one created by default. It is hosted in Azure and connects to Azure resources using public networks. Its location is set automatically; we do not have any control over it.

This type of runtime is fully managed by Azure. There's nothing to install or worry about.

Self-hosted runtime

If we want to avoid public networks while interacting with cloud or on-premises data stores, we must use this type of runtime. It consists of a service that is installed on a machine on our domain. This machine must have access to the data that we want to access from ADF. The data could be in any on-premise data store, like SQL Server, Oracle, CSV files, and so on. Basically, a self-hosted runtime is a gateway that allows ADF to connect to data on a private network.

In future examples, we'll copy data from `WWImportersDW` to an Azure storage account. We'll use this runtime to access the data in our SQL Server on Windows.

SSIS integration runtime

This runtime is specifically used to execute SSIS in the cloud. This is what we're going to use in the remainder of this chapter. It allows for the creation of an integration catalog in an Azure database, and we can therefore deploy our packages into it.

Once the catalog is created, we can configure the runtime to scale out package execution to multiple workers in Azure. This means that if your package calls can be executed in parallel, they can be executed on different compute services, which increases load performance.

Adding an SSIS integration runtime to the factory

We'll now add an integration runtime:

1. First, we'll go back into our factory, click on **Pipelines | Connections**, and then click on **Integration Runtimes** at the top, as shown in the following screenshot:

Factory blade (ADFV2Book) Connections setting

An Azure integration runtime is present, since the data factory can connect to cloud services by default.

2. To add a new integration runtime, we click on the **+ New** icon above the integration runtime **Name** column. **Integration Runtime Setup** appears. There are two different integration runtimes that can be created: self-hosted and SSIS.

3. Select **Lift-and-Shift existing SSIS packages to execute in Azure,** and click on **Next**:

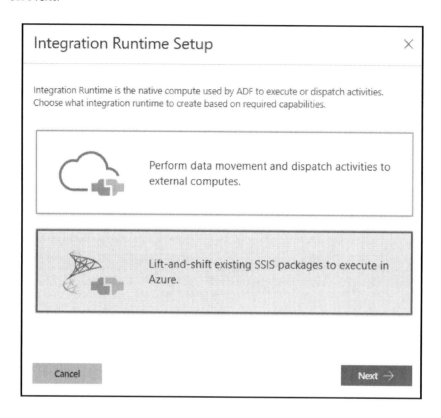

4. The first step is to fill in the general settings, as shown in the following screenshot:

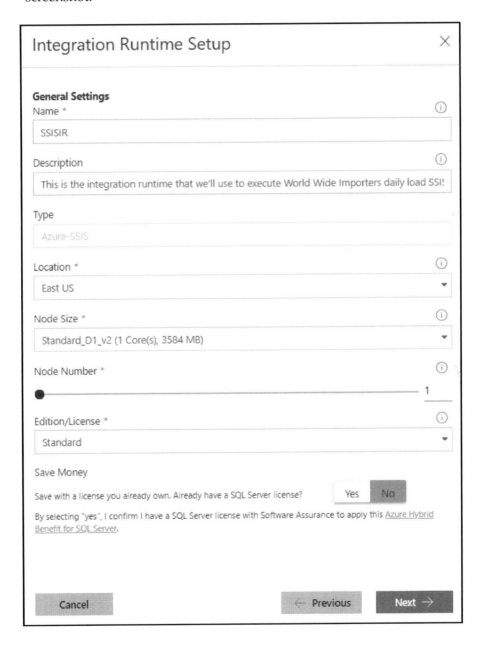

Some properties are worth explaining:

- **Name and Description**: There are no special Azure rules here. We can use the name we want.
- **Location**: Choose a location that is the same as, or very close to, your SQL Azure database, to minimize cross location traffic, and therefore, costs.
- **Node Size**: This is the size of the virtual machine that will be created to load the SSIS package(s). In our case, the package is very small; we'll therefore use the smallest available VM size.
- **Node Number**: This is an important property when we know that our packages can run in parallel. In our case, there is only a single package call. We can therefore set this property to **1**. Bear in mind that the more nodes you use, the more VMs will be used, and this has a consequence on the cost of the runtime in Azure.
- **Edition/License**: This is the SQL Server SSISDB edition. In our case, we'll use the standard edition. If we were using enterprise features like fuzzy lookups in SSIS, we would have to choose the Enterprise Edition.

The last feature asks us whether we want to use our own licenses. If you have SQL Server Software Assurance, you can select this feature. Click **Next**:

- **SQL Settings**: We'll tell the integration runtime where to create the SSISDB catalog database. We'll use the database that we created in the first chapter of this book:

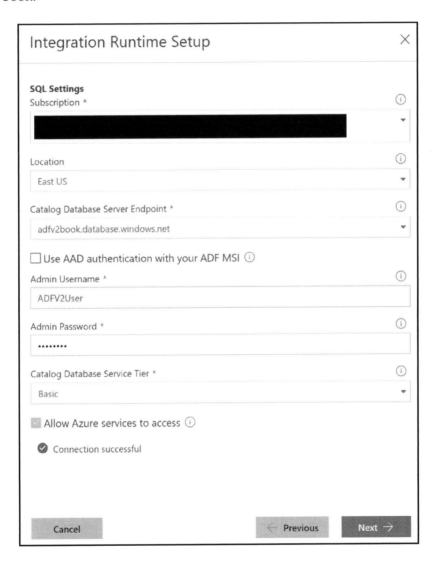

- **Subscription**: The Azure subscription that you use to do the exercises in this book.
- **Location**: This involves the same recommendations as the previous screen. It should be in the same region as the one chosen for the SSIS integration runtime.
- **Catalog Database Server Endpoint**: This is your Azure SQL Server, where the SSIS catalog (SSISDB) will be created.
- **Use AAD authentication with your ADF MSI**: Use this if you have configured **AAD** (short for **Active Directory Admin**) login in your database server. In our case, we haven't done it, so we'll specify a user and password instead.
- **Admin Username/Password**: This is the Azure SQL Server that has admin privileges to create the SSISDB database.
- **Catalog Database Service Tier**: We use the Basic tier, since we don't foresee a lot of workload when our package executes. We would choose another tier if we had a lot of workload, to reduce contention on our SSISDB database.

Now, click on **Test**. If everything works well, you should get the message **Connection successful**, and the **Test** button should change to **Next**. Click on **Next** to get to the advanced settings.

There is not much to configure here:

- **Maximum Parallel Execution Per Node**: We'll leave the default (**1**), since we have only a single package to execute. We would use a greater number if we had a bigger workload of packages.
- **Custom Setup Container SAS URI**: If we wanted to customize our SSISDB deployment, we would specify the location of the script to run.
- **Select a VNet...**: If we are using a virtual network, we check this property to enter the details of it. In our case, we'll leave it unchecked, since we made our database available in the public network. But, if you cannot do it, check this box, and enter the VNet details.

Click on **Finish**. The integration runtime creates an integration services catalog on our Azure SQL Server and starts the worker node, as shown in the following screenshot. It may take up to 30 minutes to complete. Once it completes, the status changes to **Running**:

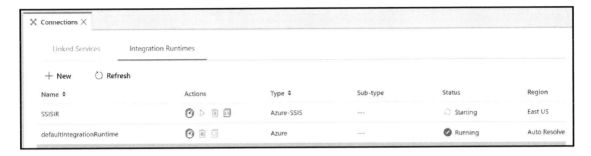

We'll now connect to our Azure SQL Server SSISDB database. Start SSMS, and enter your credentials. Click on **Options**:

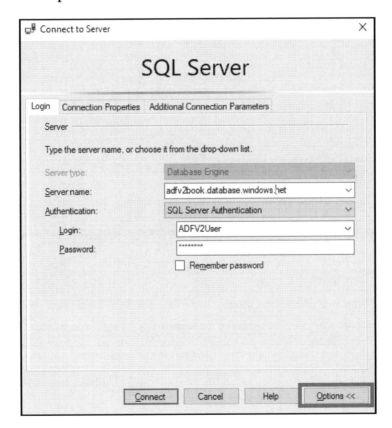

To be able to see the SSIS catalog, we need to tell SSMS that we want to connect to SSISDB. To do so, click on **Connection Properties**, and type `SSISDB` in the textbox beside **Connect to database**. Once this is done, click on **Connect**:

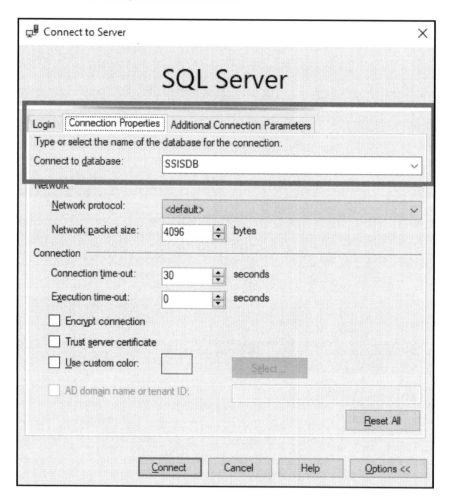

Now, expand the SSISDB node in the SSMS's object explorer, right-click on it, and choose **Create Folder...**. Enter the information, as shown in the following screenshot, and click on **OK**:

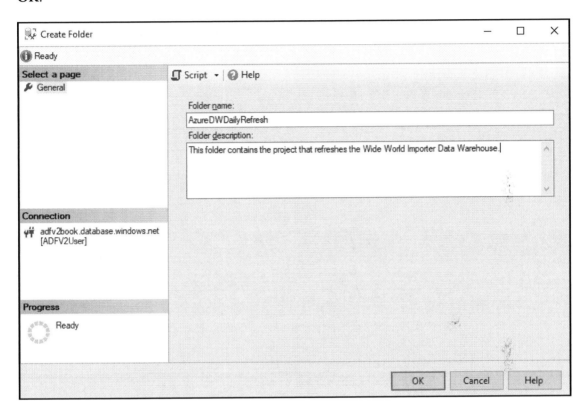

The folder gets created.

Now, let's switch to SSDT and deploy the project by right-clicking on it and choosing to **Deploy**. When we get to the **Select Destination** screen of the wizard, we'll connect to the Azure database where we created the SSIS integration runtime. As shown in the following screenshot, enter the database information, choose **SQL Server Authentication** as the **Authentication** method, and click on the **Connect** button to connect to the Azure database. Then, change the path to which the project gets deployed by using the **Browse...** button. Once that is done, click on **Next**:

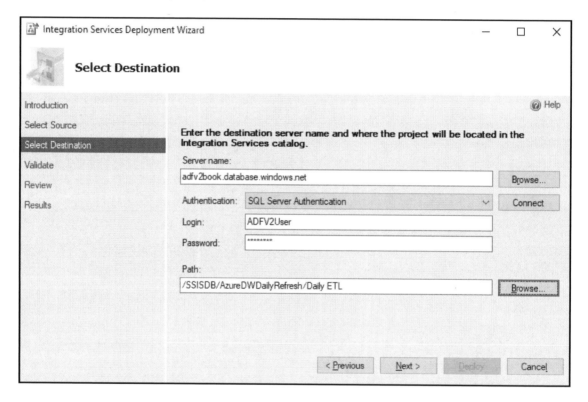

In the **Validate** step, we get some warnings, because we are using connections that connect to on-premises databases, as shown in the following screenshot. This means that the wizard cannot validate that the ADF will be able to connect to our on-premises database. We'll take care of this later; for now, click **Next**:

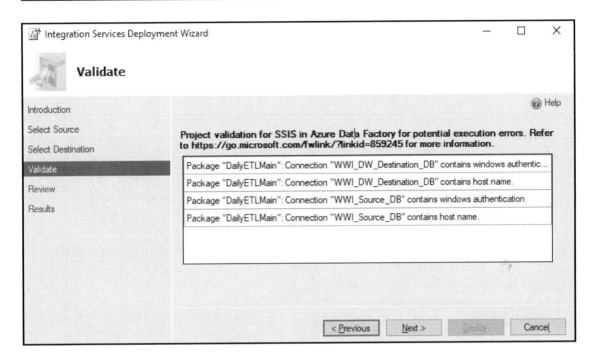

At the last page of the wizard, click **Deploy** to deploy the project to the SSIS integration runtime.

We have successfully deployed our project in the SSIS integration runtime. Now, let's test it. We go back to SSMS, and, connected to our Azure database, we enter the following command into the query editor window:

```
CATALOG.set_execution_credential @user=<Your Windows login user to access
the on-premise database>, @domain=<Your domain>, @password=<Your windows
login password>
```

Then, to verify that the information is correctly entered, we can check it by using the following SQL syntax:

```
SELECT *
FROM CATALOG.master_properties
WHERE property_name = 'EXECUTION_DOMAIN' OR property_name =
'EXECUTION_USER'
```

This command sets the credentials that will allow the SSIS integration runtime to use Windows authentication with our SQL Server database. Basically, it will get rid of the warning that we had at validation time, when we deployed the project.

We can now test our package deployed in the SSIS integration runtime. In SSMS, navigate to **Daily** and right-click on **Execute**. The **Execute Package** wizard screen appears, as shown in the following screenshot. Click on **OK** to start the execution:

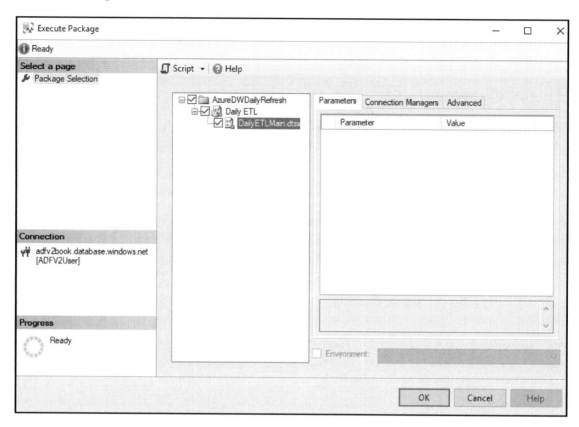

Click on **OK** to see the execution report. After 1-2 minutes, the package should finish its execution successfully. If not, look at the messages and fix any errors. From that point, the worst is done (in a sense), and ADF will now call this package using the same credentials.

SSIS execution from a pipeline

Now, let's go back into our factory. As shown in the following screenshot, click on the + sign and choose pipeline from the contextual menu that appears. Rename it from `pipeline1` to `MainPilelineADFV2Book`. Drag and drop an **Execute SSIS Package** activity on the pipeline area:

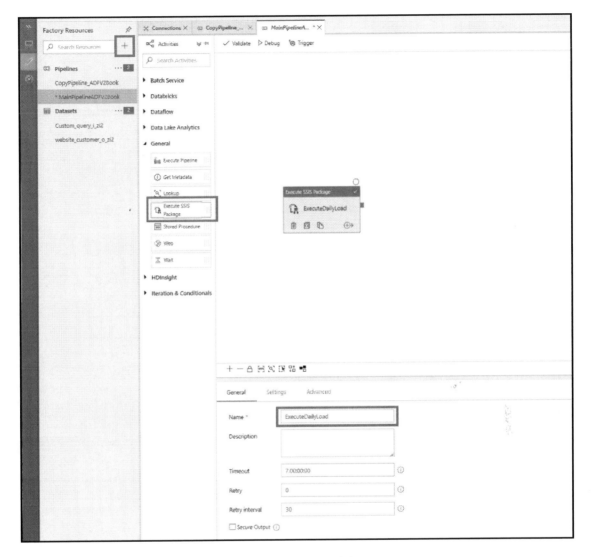

Factory blade (pipeline execution)

Click on the activity, make sure that the **General** tab is selected, and rename it
ExecuteDailyLoad, as shown in the preceding screenshot.

Click on the **Setting** tab and set the properties to those shown in the following screenshot:

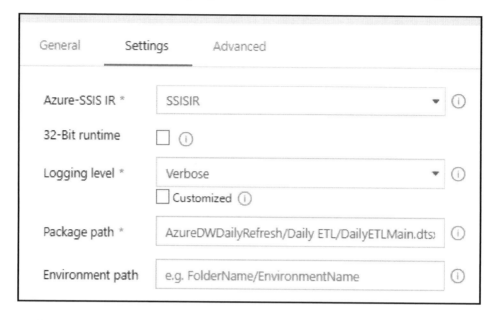

- **Azure-SSIS IR**: Select **SSISIR** from the drop-down list.
- **32-Bit runtime**: Let it uncheck.
- **Logging level**: Choose **Verbose** from the drop-down list. We want to get the maximum information available in the SSIS logs, in case an error occurs.
- **Package path**: Type `AzureDWDailyRefresh/Daily ETL/DailyETLMain.dtsx`.
- **Environment path**: We're not using any environments; leave this textbox empty.

We're finished setting up the activity. We can now click on **Debug**, at the top of the pipeline window, to do a dry run of our package execution. Once we do it, the **Execute SSIS Package** activity gets a yellow icon, to indicate that it's executing. Also, the execution run's details appear at the bottom of the screen:

Once the execution has finished, we can see that it worked properly, as shown in the following screenshot:

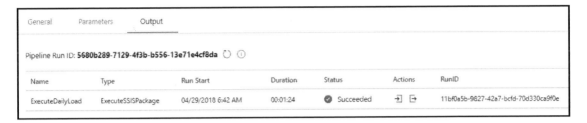

That's it! We're able to call the data warehouse refresh from SSIS. Now, let's publish our pipeline to save it in ADF. Click the **Publish All** button to publish the newly created pipeline:

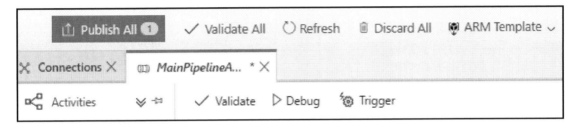

Summary

That was a pretty long journey, but we made it!

The most complex step is done now. In this chapter, we saw how SSIS can interact with Azure. We built services for integrating data using ADF V2. We're also able to refresh on-premises data from ADF in the cloud. In the next chapters, we'll add activities to this pipeline.

4
Azure Data Lake

One of the biggest problems that mid enterprise-sized organizations face is that data resides everywhere. Over the years, data has been accumulated usually by different systems, third-party, or in-house developed applications. Many vendors have set up a requirement to segregate their database servers in order to ensure performance, security, and management of their systems. Also, third-party vendors did not or do not want to take responsibility for their systems in a shared environment.

Organizations are starting to realize, or are already in the process of realizing, that consolidation is a must, both from the cost perspective as well as for easier manageability. However, in many cases, the vendors or developers are no longer to be found, which makes it very hard to make decisions to upgrade and/or migrate to the cloud. What could complicate things even further is the fact that shared or centralized data may be replicated everywhere and there may not even be one source of truth for the centralized data.

The bottom line is that if you have managed to complete a successful consolidation project with one source of truth, you are lucky and one of the few who have been able to achieve this goal!

On the other hand, it's the era of data analytics and reports, spanning multiple systems. Single sources of the truth are becoming more and more important. There are huge amounts of data to scan, summarize, analyze...

And so Microsoft came up with the Azure Data Lake, which is, in a nutshell, a cloud offering for big data that integrates with other Azure services such as: SQL database, SQL Server, SQL data warehouse, machine learning, Power BI, and Cortana. It also allows us to import and export data from almost any data source. Its main goals are ease of use and cost-effectiveness. The service has two main components:

- Data Lake Store (static)
- Data Lake Analytics component (paid on demand)

According to Microsoft at `https://azure.microsoft.com/en-ca/solutions/data-lake/`:

"The Azure Data Lake includes all the capabilities required to make it easy for developers, data scientists, and analysts to store data of any size, shape, and speed, and do all types of processing and analytics across platforms and languages. It removes the complexities of ingesting and storing all of your data while making it faster to get up and running with batch, streaming, and interactive analytics. Azure Data Lake works with existing IT investments for identity, management, and security for simplified data management and governance. It also integrates seamlessly with operational stores and data warehouses so you can extend current data applications. We've drawn on the experience of working with enterprise customers and running some of the largest scale processing and analytics in the world for Microsoft businesses like Office 365, Xbox Live, Azure, Windows, Bing, and Skype. Azure Data Lake solves many of the productivity and scalability challenges that prevent you from maximizing the value of your data assets with a service that's ready to meet your current and future business needs."

This chapter will primarily focus on the components of the Azure Data Lake and basic implementation of those components.

 While the examples in this chapter will give you an overview of typical scenarios, we encourage you to adapt this proposal according to your needs.

We will cover the following:

- Creating and configuring the Data Lake Store resource
- Creating and configuring the Data Lake Analytics resource
- Using data factory to create and configure Data Lake Store/Analytics
- Uploading data from an SQL Server Azure VM database into the data lake using blob storage
- Calling a U-SQL script to summarize data into a new file in the data lake using blob storage (this part requires Data Lake Analytics)
- Running U-SQL from a Data Lake Analytics job to do the following point
- Summarizing data into a new file in the data lake using blob storage (this part requires Data Lake Analytics)

Creating and configuring Data Lake Store

We will first create and configure the Data Lake Store:

1. Open the Azure Portal. If you are just starting, you will not see any resource configured under the **All resources** and **ALL SUBSCRIPTIONS** section:

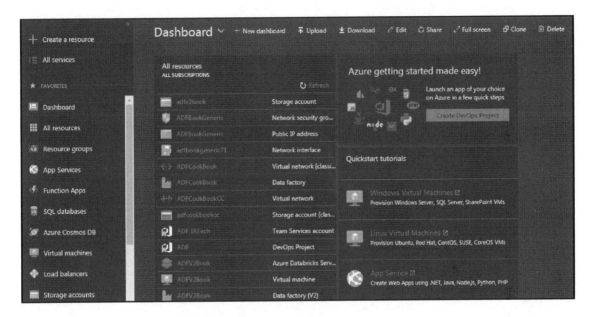

2. On the top left, click on **Create a resource**; enter the words Data Lake in **Search the Marketplace**:

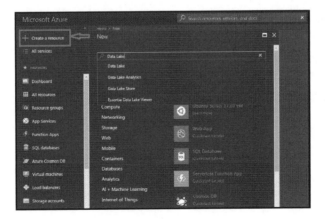

3. Select **Data Lake Store** from the list (third option in the image) if you have no Data Lake stores yet; the following screen will open up:

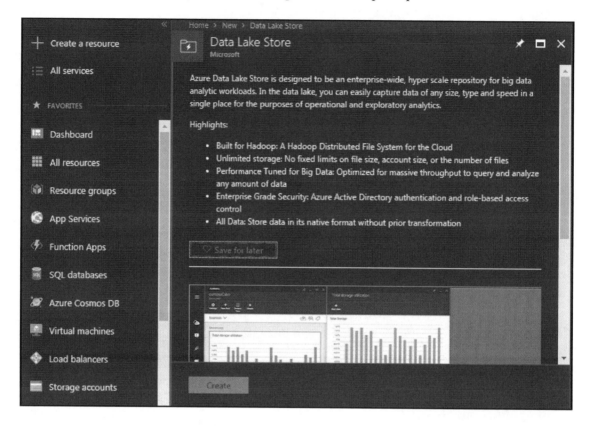

4. Select **Create**.
5. Enter the details of the Data Lake. Note that the name has to be all lowercase and with no special characters. You will get a message as you type if you've entered any incorrect character. In this case, we are not using any encryption, for simplicity. Note that the default is encryption enabled. For more information about the encryption options, see `Encryption of data in Azure Data Lake Store` (`https://docs.microsoft.com/en-us/azure/data-lake-store/data-lake-store-get-started-portal`).

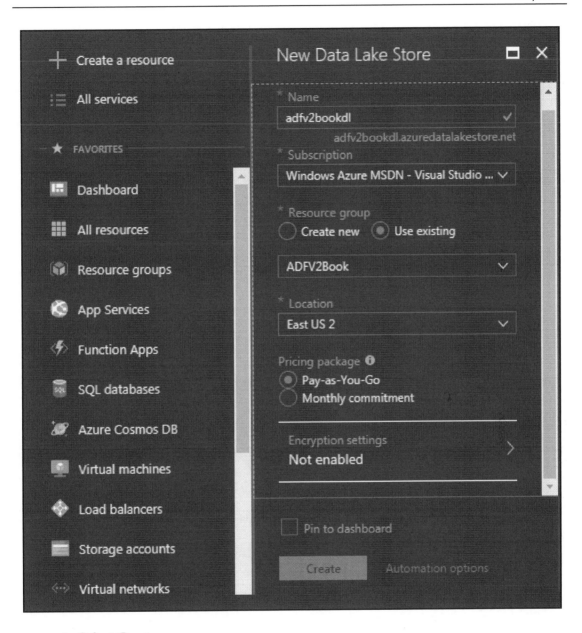

6. Select **Create**.

7. Once the Data Lake is created, you will see it in the list of resources:

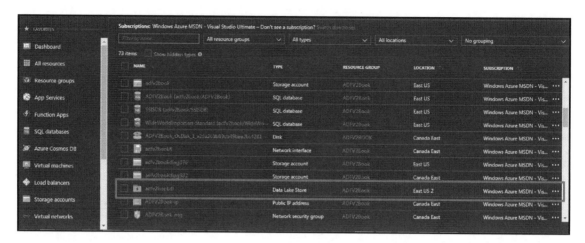

List of resources (Data Lake Store)

8. Click on the resource to open it. Something like this will open, where you can change the properties as you wish:

9. Congratulations! A Data Lake resource has been created.

Next Steps

We have created and configured a Data Lake Store. After creating the Data Lake resource, you now have the ability to upload data to it and manipulate the data using U-SQL. There will be no charge to your subscription until you actually use the Data Lake.

The next step would be to upload data to the Data Lake.

Ways to copy/import data from a database to the Data Lake

There are a few methods for copying the data from a database to the Data Lake. The main ones at the time of writing this book are:

- Using Sqoop, via a JDBC connection
- Using Data Factory
- Using SSIS

Ways to store imported data in files in the Data Lake

The options to store files in the Data Lake are:

- Using the Azure Data Lake Store File System
- HDInsight
- Blob Storage

Easily moving data to the Data Lake Store

As of May 2018, Azure Data Factory supports moving data from the following sources to the Azure Data Lake Store:

- Azure Blob
- Azure SQL Database
- Azure Table
- On-premises SQL Server Database
- Azure DocumentDB

- Azure SQL DW
- On-premises File System
- On-premises Oracle Database
- On-premises MySQL Database
- On-premises Db2 Database
- On-premises Teradata Database
- On-premises Sybase Database
- On-premises PostgreSQL Database
- On-premises HDFS
- Generic OData (coming soon!)
- Generic ODBC (coming soon!)

For an updated list of data stores that are supported as sources or sinks by the copy activity, see the supported data stores table: `https://docs.microsoft.com/en-us/azure/data-factory/copy-activity-overview#supported-data-stores-and-formats`.

Ways to directly copy files into the Data Lake

There are two options to do so:

- Upload data to **Azure Data Lake Storage (ADLS)** using **Data Explorer**
- Configure the data lake to access blob Storage

Data Explorer is a new feature that allows us to navigate ADLS resources freely. We can upload or download folders and files, copy and paste files across folders or ADLS accounts, and easily perform CRUD operations for our folders and files. Azure Storage Explorer offers a traditional desktop explorer GUI from which we can also connect to blob storage and other Azure resources. In order to connect other Azure resources, you will need to install the newest Azure Storage Explorer bits from the product web page (`https://azure.microsoft.com/features/storage-explorer/`). Azure Storage Tool will not be covered in this chapter.

It is possible to copy data from blob storage directly to the Data Lake Store using the command-line tool AdlCopy. This tool allows us to copy data from the following sources:

- From Azure Storage Blobs into Data Lake Store.
  However, you cannot use AdlCopy to copy data from Data Lake Store to Azure Storage blobs.
- Between two Azure Data Lake Store accounts.

For more information, visit `https://docs.microsoft.com/en-us/azure/data-lake-store/data-lake-store-copy-data-azure-storage-blob`

So what's next...?

- We will show you two ways to manipulate data in the Data Lake Store:
  - From a job created in the Data Lake Analytics Resource
  - From the Data Factory

Both methods require U-SQL to be executed and U-SQL requires the Data Lake Analytics.

Prerequisites for the next steps

The Data Lake resource will be created and configured from the Azure Portal. The prerequisites are:

- An Azure SQL Server instance
- A blob storage account

We have created the following view in the SQL Server database. The SQL Server Linked Service has already been created in a previous chapter:

```
CREATE VIEW ADFV2Book.Purchase AS
SELECT Dimension.Date.Date,
Dimension.Supplier.Supplier,
Dimension.Supplier.Category,
Dimension.[Stock Item].[Stock Item],
Fact.Purchase.[Ordered Quantity]
FROM Fact.Purchase
INNER JOIN Dimension.Date
ON Fact.Purchase.[Date Key] = Dimension.Date.Date
INNER JOIN Dimension.[Stock Item]
ON Fact.Purchase.[Stock Item Key] = Dimension.[Stock Item].[Stock Item Key]
INNER JOIN Dimension.Supplier
ON Fact.Purchase.[Supplier Key] = Dimension.Supplier.[Supplier Key]
```

We also need to find a container in the storage account. Click on storage accounts from the dashboard:

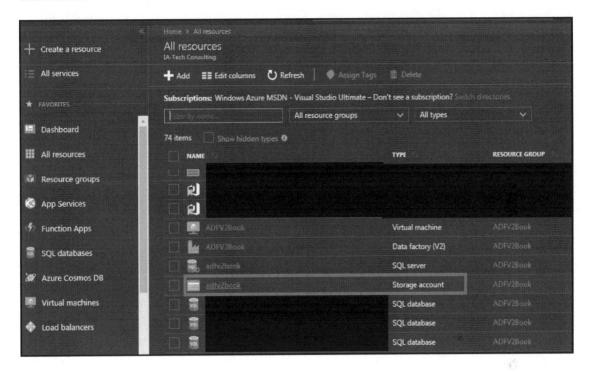

In the **Services** section, click on **Blobs**:

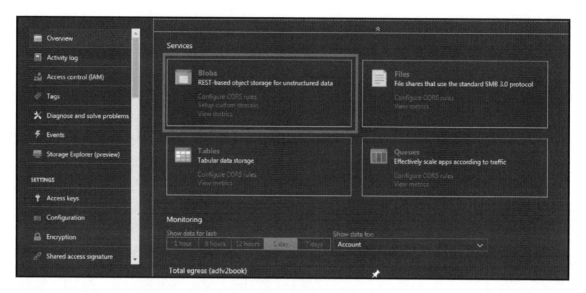

Find a container or create one (click on the **+ Container** button). We will use an existing one..

 Note that some components of the Azure Data Lake, data factory, and other Azure services/tools do not handle special characters such as blank and hyphen properly in file paths or filenames. Even though there may be ways to overcome this challenge, they may not be straightforward. We strongly recommend avoiding those special characters when handling files.

Creating a Data Lake Analytics resource

In order to be able to run a U-SQL task or job, we need to create the Data Lake Analytics resource. In the Azure dashboard, click on **New** to create a new resource and look for the **Data Lake Analytics** resource in the new window:

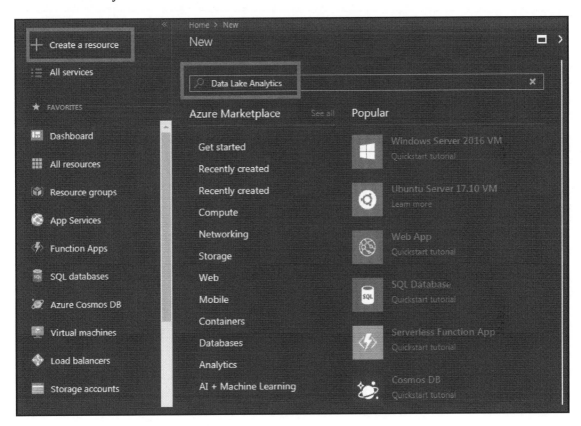

Press *Enter*, and in the new window, click on **Create**:

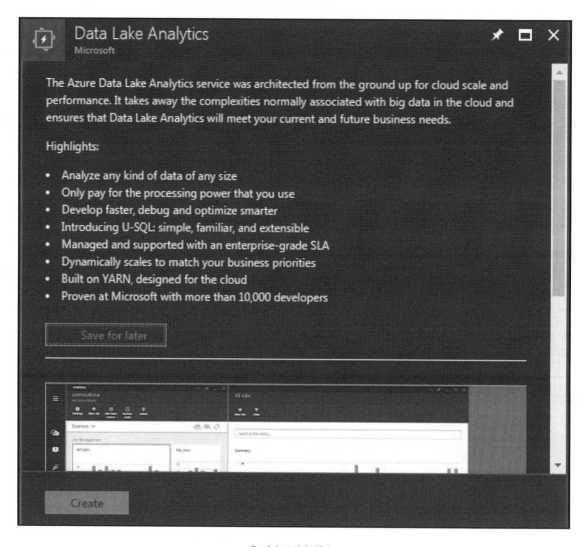

Data Lake Analytics blade

Enter the name of the new resource (note that the resource name should contain only lowercase letters and numbers) and the rest of the information:

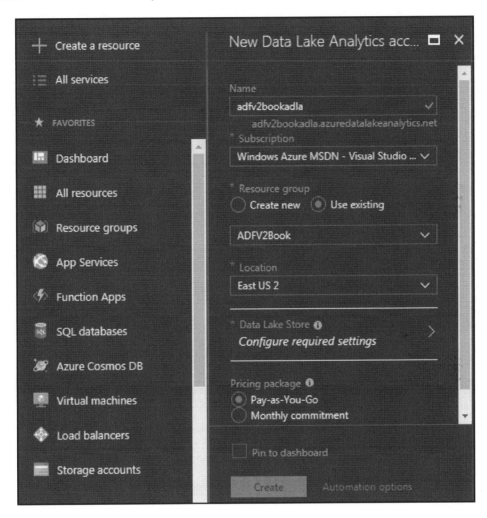

We click on the **Data Lake Store** section and choose the Data Lake Store we have previously created:

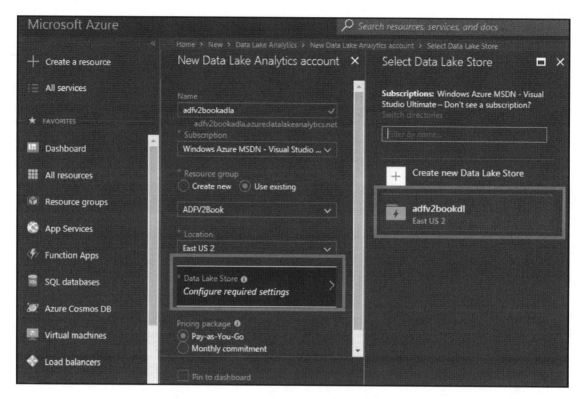

And click on **Create**:

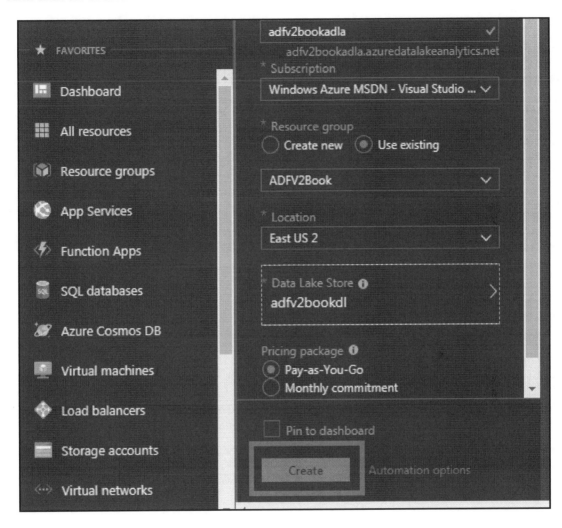

Find the new resource to ensure it was created:

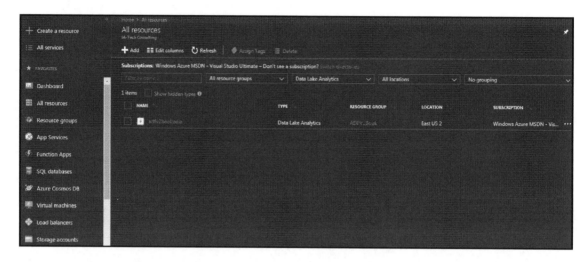

All resources blade

We have created the Data Lake Analytics resource and now we can run U-SQL to manipulate or summarize data. We can run U-SQL either directly from the Data Lake Analytics Resource, via **job**, or from the Data Factory in a **pipeline**.

The next two sections will show you how to do the following:

- Run U-SQL via a job in Data Lake Analytics to copy data from SQL Server into a blob storage file.
- Run the Copy task from the Data Factory Pipeline to do the same (copy data from SQL Server into blob Storage).
- Run another task from the data factory in the same pipeline to summarize the data from the aforementioned file into another file in blob storage.

Using the data factory to manipulate data in the Data Lake

In the previous section, we created the Data Lake Analytics Resource for the U-SQL task:

- Even though possible, it is not at all straightforward to run U-SQL to connect directly to an SQL database. It involves tweaking firewalls and permissions. This is why we do not cover this part in the next section, which describes how to run a U-SQL job directly from the Data Lake Analytics resource.
- It is much simpler to copy data from an SQL Server database to a file on Azure Blob Storage via the Azure Data Factory.
- In this section, we show how to do this and then how to manipulate the copied data with U-SQL using the Azure Data Factory.

We will now create a pipeline in Azure Data Factory that will do the following:

- **Task 1**: Import data from SQL Server (from a view) into a file on blob storage
- **Task 2**: Use U-SQL to export summary data to a file on blob storage

Task 1 – copy/import data from SQL Server to a blob storage file using data factory

Let's create a data factory pipeline and a task to copy the data from the SQL Server to a blob storage file. From the **Dashboard**, click on the data factory:

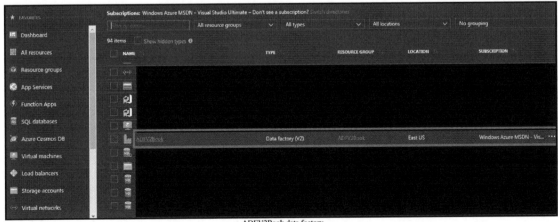

ADFV2Book data factory

After clicking on the data factory, the following window opens. Click on the + to create a new factory resource and choose **Pipeline**:

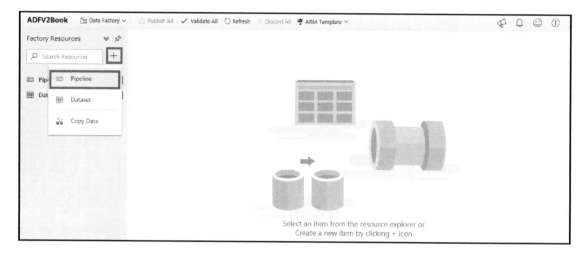

Configure the new pipeline (name and description):

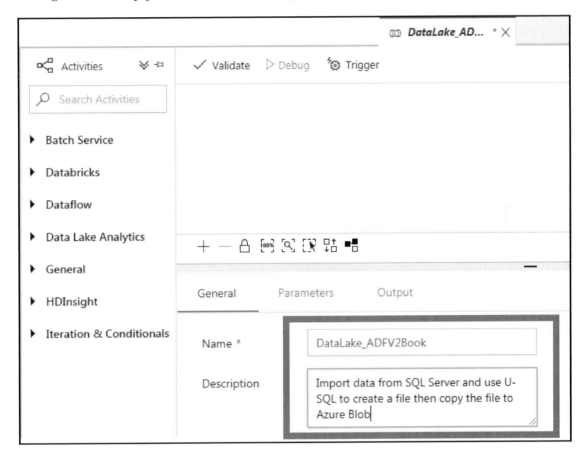

Expand the **Dataflow** section:

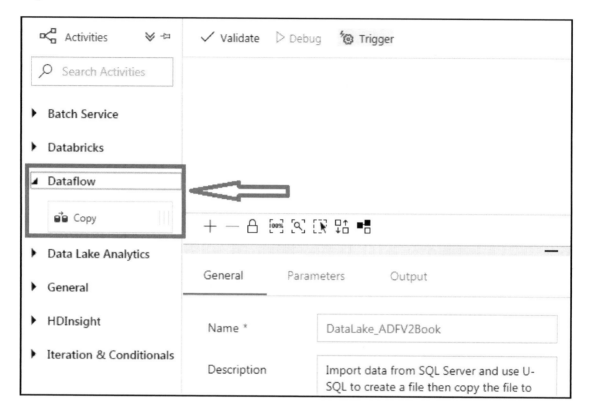

Drag and drop the **Copy** task into the window, and change its name:

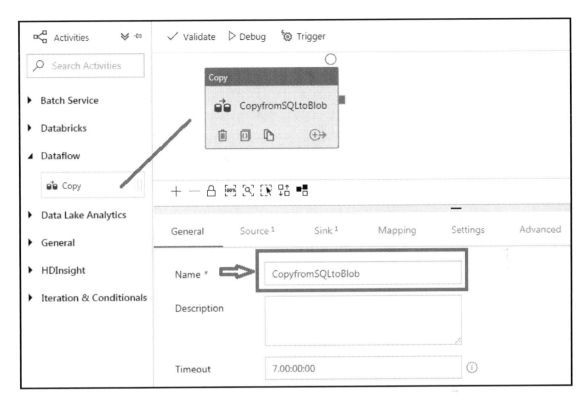

In the **Source** tab, click on **New**:

In **Select a Data Store**, write `sql`; choose your source type and **Finish**.

We are using an Azure SQL Server instance in this example.

In the **Connection** tab, select the relevant SQL Database connection in **Linked service** (note that the connection has already been defined in the **Connections** sections previously):

And then select the table/view (in our case, we select the `View ADFV2Book.Purchase`):

You can preview the data to ensure all is good by pressing on **Preview data**. Note that a new SQLServerPurchaseView dataset has been created:

Back at the pipeline, you can modify the dataset to a query or stored procedure:

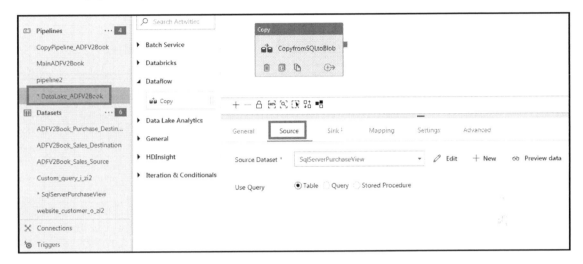

In the **Sink** tab, choose **New** for sink dataset and look for `blob`. Choose the **Azure Blob Storage**:

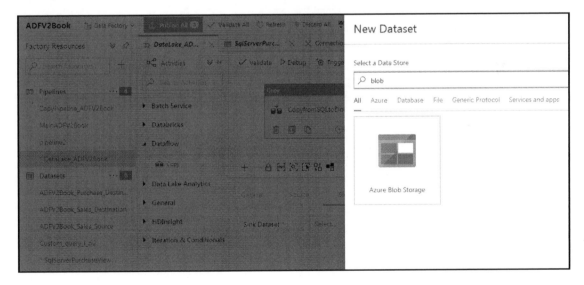

We modify the name of the Azure Blob Storage we will be using.

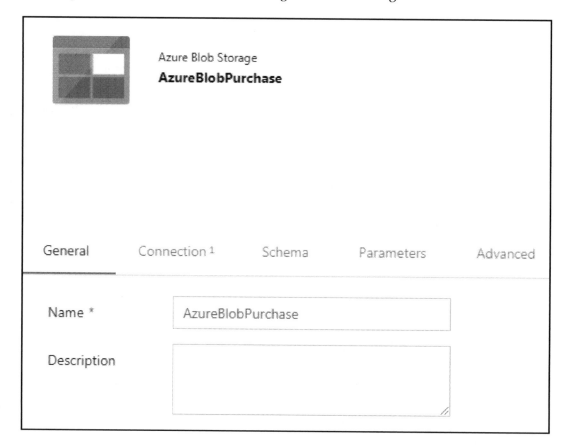

In the **Connection** section, we choose to create a New Linked Service to create the blob storage file that we need to export the data to:

Enter the details in the **New Linked Service** window, starting with the name:

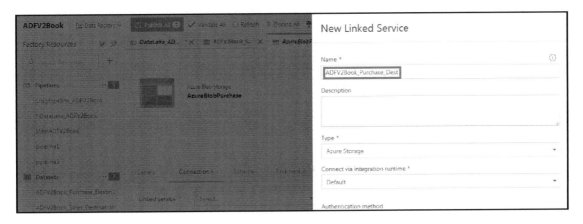

In the **Account selection method**, you can choose **From Azure subscription**; the Azure subscription details will be automatically populated. Also add the **Storage account name** (of the blob storage you already have):

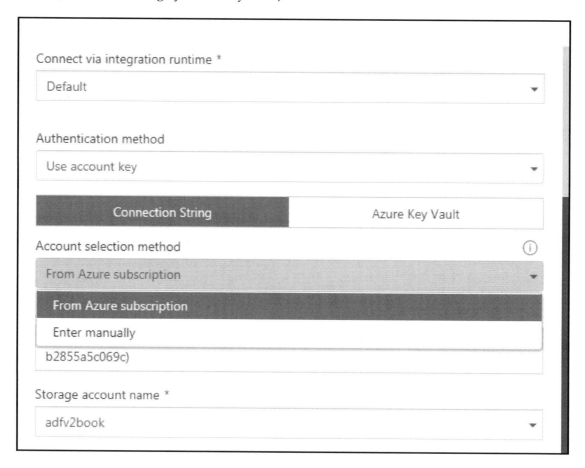

Click **Test connection** at the bottom, and if it's successful, click on **Finish**:

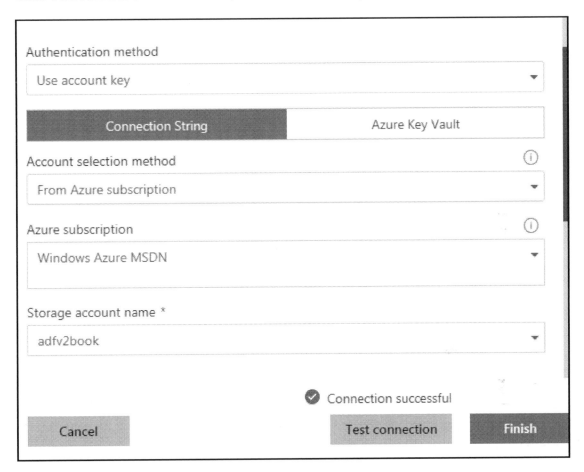

In the file path, you can either choose a hardcoded name or go for **Dynamic content** (*Alt +P*) to create a dynamic filename, for example, with the date extension.

Note that if you do not state a hard coded filename, the name will be `[DBSchemaName].[DBTableName].txt`.

The `[]` brackets may cause issues in some components, so we strongly recommend that you use filenames without them. In our example, the file name will be hardcoded as `ADFVV2BookPurchaseData.csv`:

Scroll down and choose the file format and properties. If your file contains a character in the column values themselves, it cannot be the delimiter. In our case here, some string columns contain commas (,). Therefore, I have chosen t (**Tab**) to be the delimiter.

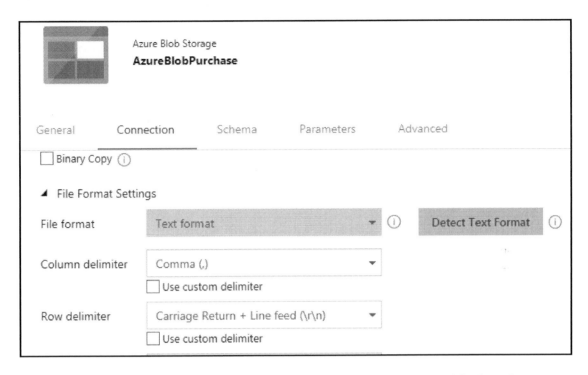

In the **Schema** tab, click on the **Import Schema** button and you can modify the column names accordingly; however, you do not need to do so. We will be doing this in the pipeline task.

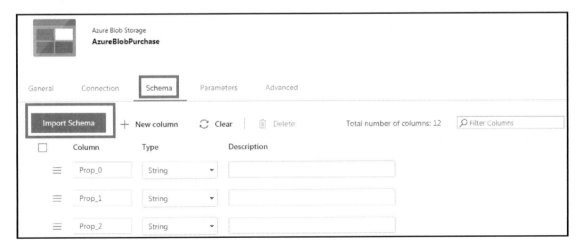

It is extremely important to ensure that the number of columns here is the same as the column number in the SQL Server view or table in the Source (otherwise, the task may fail with an error related to the number of columns not matching).

When done, you need to use **Publish All** in order to save the changes:

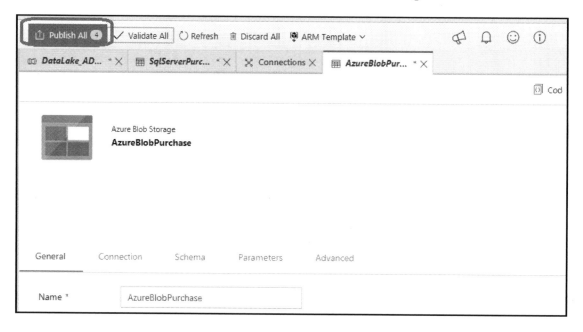

Reopen the pipeline and open the **Mapping** tab; you should see the column names from the view. If not, you can reimport the schemas or add them manually:

If required (that is, there is a number of unpublished changes), select **Publish All** again. After publishing all changes, click on **Validate** to validate the task. This should be successful!

In order to run the task, you should click on **Trigger**. Once it has executed successfully, you may go to the blob storage container again and click on the container.

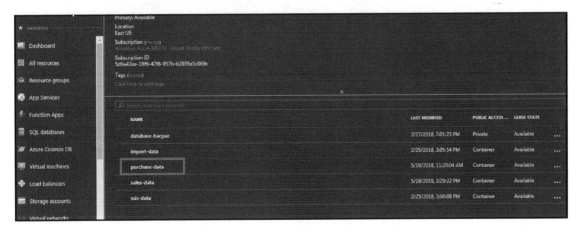

Purchase-data container

You should see your file in there (and on top of it, you can see how the format of the filename will look if you do not specify a filename):

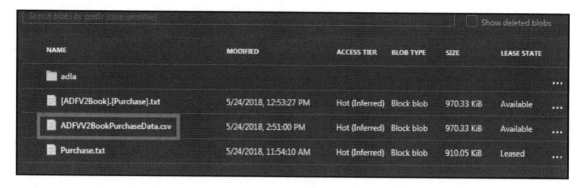

We double-click on the file and copy the URL somewhere, as we will need to use it later when writing the U-SQL:

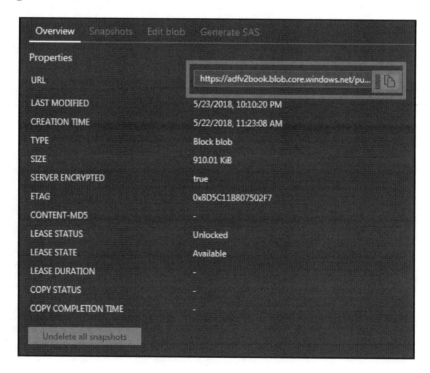

We have created a data factory pipeline with a copy task, where the source is a view that was created in an SQL Server database. The destination for the data copy is a file in a blob storage folder.

The next step would be to add a U-SQL task to manipulate the data in this created file, by summarizing data and copying the results to a new file in the blob storage.

Task 2 – run a U-SQL task from the data factory pipeline to summarize data

So here's the deal... The best way to create and debug a U-SQL script is to run it directly from a Data Lake Analytics job. We suggest you read/implement what's written in the next section (run U-SQL from a job in the Data Lake Analytics) before you continue here. In the next section, you will find all the configurations that are required to run U-SQL as well as the U-SQL script itself.

So here is a placeholder for you to come back to read this section

We will use the same pipeline we have previously created to add a U-SQL task for data manipulation in the data lake. Reopen the pipeline and open the **Data Lake Analytics** activity. Then drag and drop the **U-SQL** task:

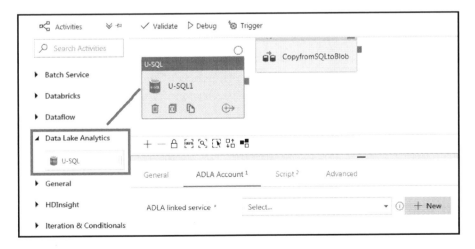

You can modify the name of the U-SQL:

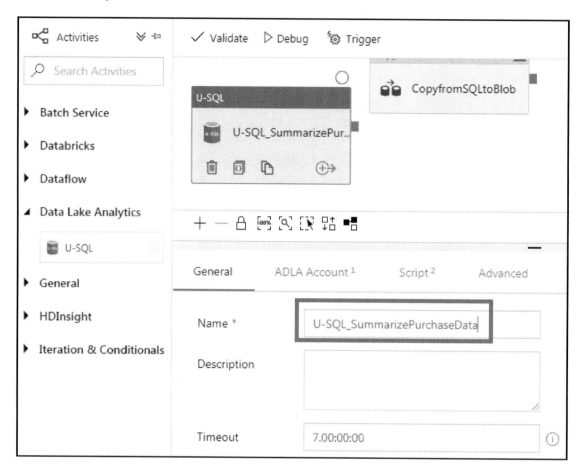

Next, in the U-SQL task, click on the **ADLA Account** tab and click on **New**:

A new window will open; you may change the name of the new ADLA linked service and choose the new Data Lake Analytics resource.

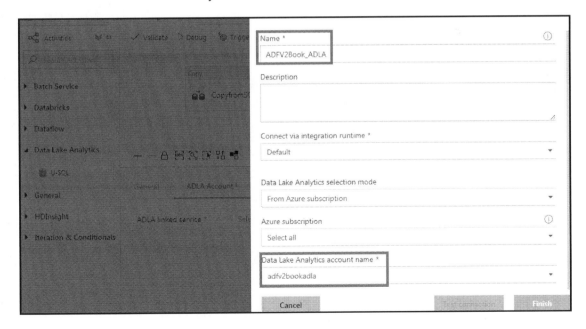

ADLA resource blade

Scroll down. The tenant ID will be automatically populated. The **Service Principal ID** needs to be filled in. Details are at `https://docs.microsoft.com/en-us/azure/data-factory/transform-data-using-data-lake-analytics#azure-data-lake-analytics-linked-service`.

Service principal authentication

Azure Data Lake Store uses Azure Active Directory for authentication. Before authoring an application that works with Azure Data Lake Store, you must decide how to authenticate your application with **Azure Active Directory (Azure AD)**. The two main options available are:

- End-user authentication
- Service-to-service authentication

Both these options result in your application being provided with an OAuth 2.0 token, which gets attached to each request made to Azure Data Lake Store.

We have created the end-user authentication method by following this link: `https://docs.microsoft.com/en-us/azure/azure-resource-manager/resource-group-create-service-principal-portal`. The user creating it should be configured as the owner of the resource and also as an admin in the active directory resource.

In the Azure portal, inside all resources, click on the **Azure Active Directory** resource:

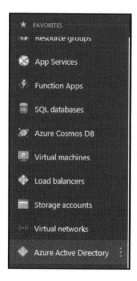

Click on **App registrations** and **New application registration**:

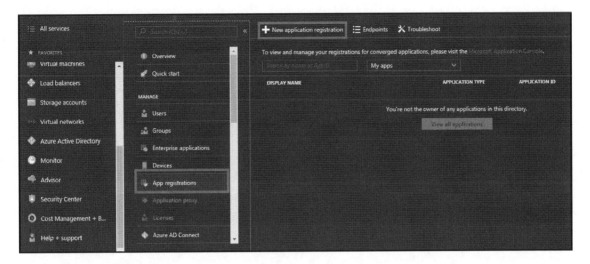

Provide a name and URL for the application. **Select Web app / API** for the type of application you want to create and click on **Create**. The URL will look something like this: `https://<your domain>.com/ADFV2BookApp`.

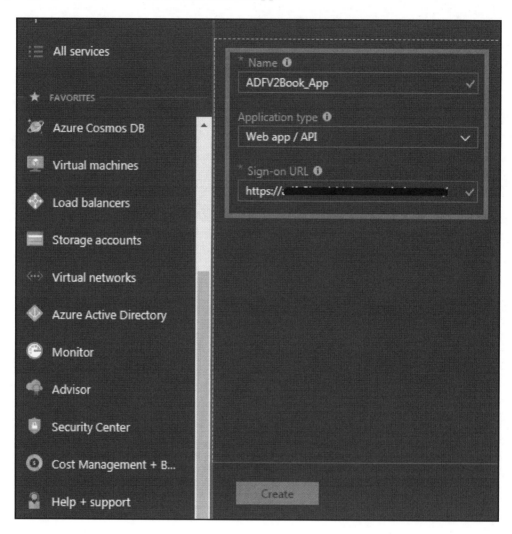

Once the application is registered, we need to grant it permissions on the Blob Storage and the Azure Data Lake Analytics resource. Open **Data Lake Analytics Resource | Access Control IAM** and add the application as a contributor:

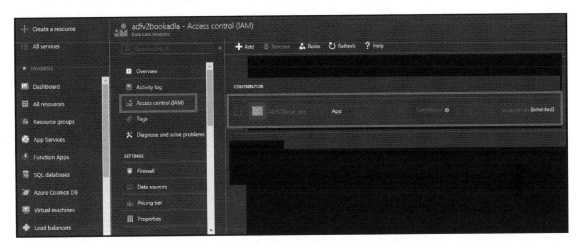

Similarly for the Blob Storage: open the **Blob Storage Resource | Access Control IAM** and add the application as a contributor.

So now we are ready to add the U-SQL task. Go back to the new pipeline and move the U-SQL task to the right; drag the arrow from the copy task to the U-SQL task:

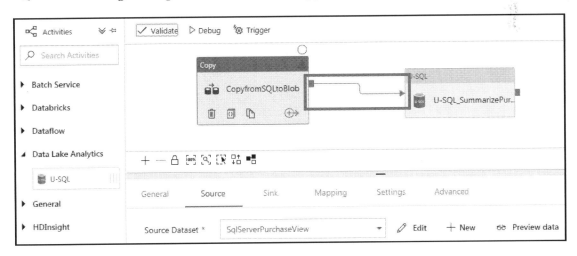

Click on the U-SQL task and choose the new ADLA linked service. Test the connection; it should be successful:

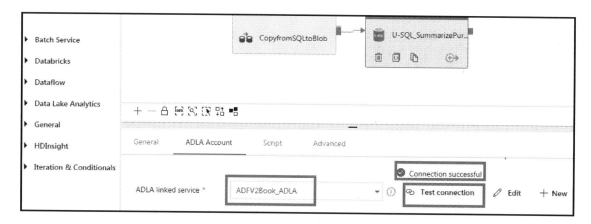

In the **Script** tab, you can either load a script from the blob storage or from your local machine. The script should be the same one as we have previously used.

In our case, the U-SQL script described in the next section is saved on the blob Storage, so we are choosing the blob storage and then loading the script to the task. Make sure that the script was tested so that it does not fail.

You can validate, debug, and publish changes:

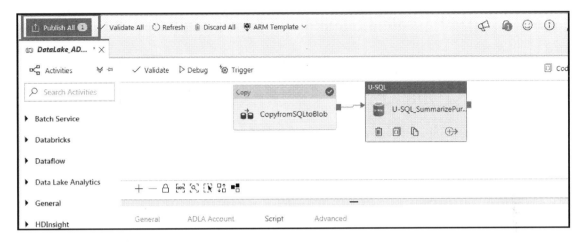

Ensure that it runs successfully. You can check it from the notification icon on the top right:

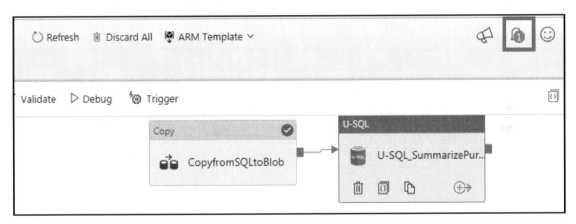

The last step is to verify that the output file was created. You can do that by opening the **Blob Storage Resource | Storage Explorer**.

Run U-SQL from a job in the Data Lake Analytics

In this section, we will learn how to create a Data Lake Analytics job that will debug and run a U-SQL script. This job will summarize data from the file created by Task 1 in the preceding data factory pipeline (the task that imports SQL Server data into a blob file). The summary data will be copied to a new file on the blob storage.

With U-SQL, we can join different blob files and manipulate/summarize the data. We can also import data from different data sources. However, in this section, we will only provide a very basic U-SQL as an example.

Let's get started...

First, we open the Data Lake Analytics resource from the dashboard. We first need to add the Blob Storage account here. Open **Data sources**:

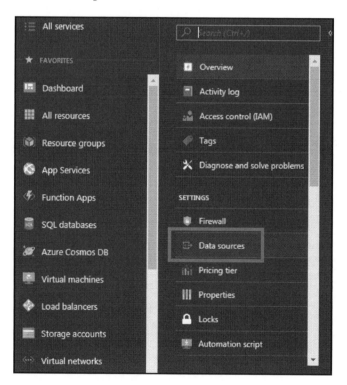

Click on **Add data source**:

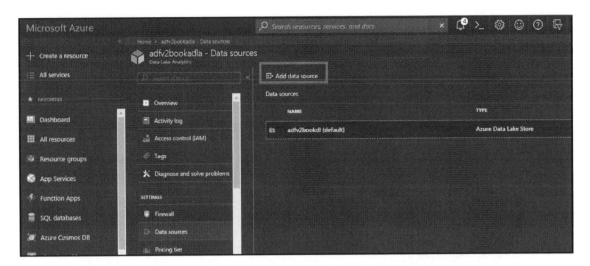

Fill in the details:

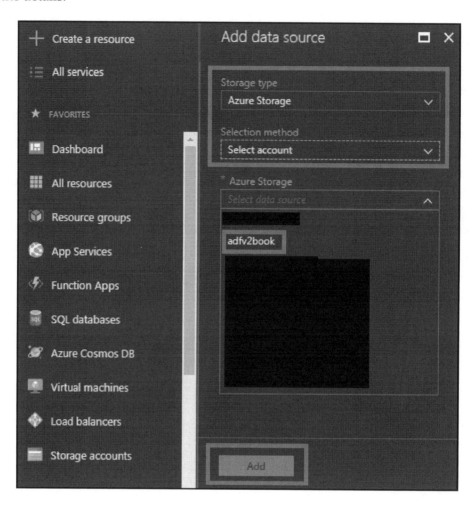

You should see the added blob storage in the list:

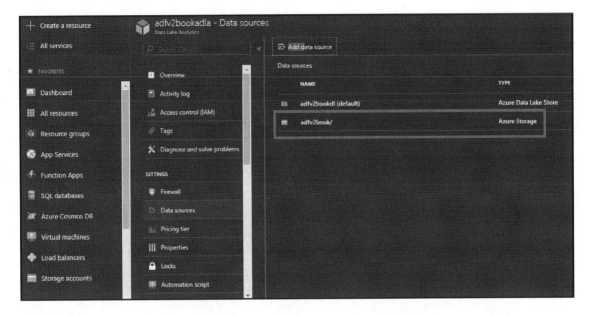

You can explore the containers in the blob storage and files from the **Data Lake Analytics** | **Data explorer**:

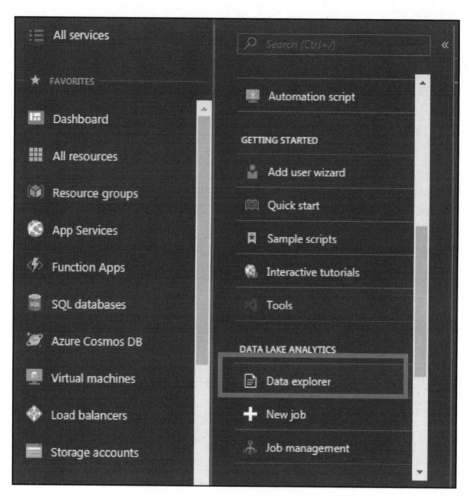

Click on **Data explorer**:

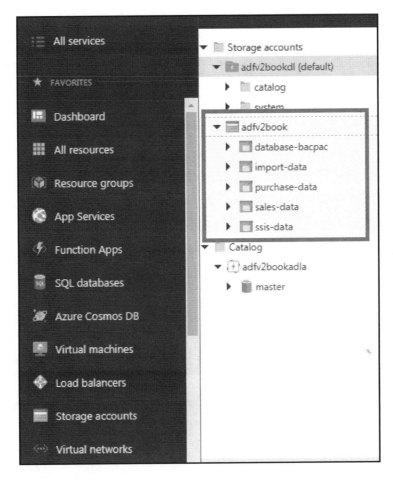

In order to get the path, you can click on the container and then copy the **WASB PATH**, either for the container or the file itself. By clicking on the file, you can find the path in the **Properties**.

Do not copy a URL from the blob storage resource (only from the Data Lake Analytics), as it will not give you the **WASB PATH**.

Next, we will add the SQL Server as a data source as well.

So now we can click on **New job** from the Data Lake Analytics page to add a job that will execute a U-SQL:

Data Lake Analytics blade (creating new job)

Create the job with the U-SQL code. You may **Save** it; the U-SQL code will appear as a file in the **Downloads** of your browser.

You need to **Submit** it in order to run the job:

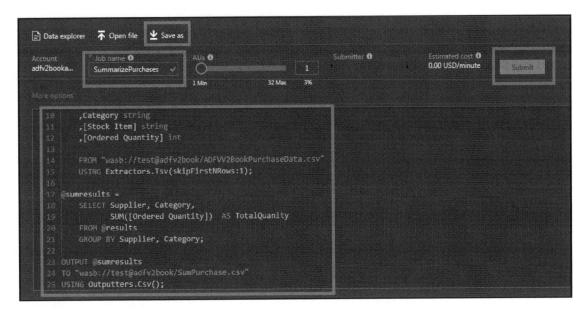

Here is the U-SQL code example (use the container or filename URL you have previously copied in the script as the input file):

```
@results = EXTRACT
Date DateTime
,Supplier string
,Category string
,[Stock Item] string
,[Ordered Quantity] int

FROM "wasb://purchase-data@adfv2book/ADFV2BookPurchaseData.csv"
USING Extractors.Tsv(skipFirstNRows:1); //Skip header row

@sumresults =SELECT Supplier, Category,
SUM([Ordered Quantity]) AS TotalQuanity
FROM @results
GROUP BY Supplier, Category;

OUTPUT @sumresults
TO "wasb://purchase-data@adfv2book/SumPurchase.csv"
USING Outputters.Csv();
```

At the end of the run, this is what you wish to see:

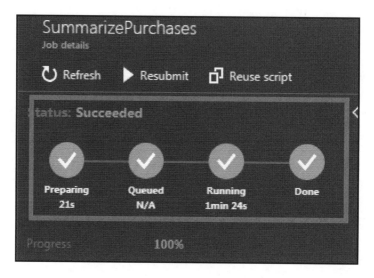

Summary

In this chapter we saw the components of the Azure Data Lake and basic implementation of those components.

Machine Learning on the Cloud

5

Machine learning is the ability of a machine to expand its knowledge without human intervention. The concept of machine learning is used in software engineering, in data mining, and, in particular, in artificial intelligence. Starting from a knowledge base rich in information, an automatic learning system searches and extracts any regularity between data through data mining techniques. Machine learning algorithms use mathematical-computational methods to learn information directly from the data, without mathematical models and predetermined equations.

The applications of machine learning are already numerous today, some of which have commonly entered our daily life without us realizing it. For example, search engines, through one or more keywords, return lists of results. Spam filters of emails continuously learn both to intercept suspicious or fraudulent email messages and to act accordingly. Finally, we have speech recognition systems or manual writing identification.

In this chapter, we will be introduced to the basic concepts of machine learning, and then we will take a tour of different types of algorithms. In addition, an introduction, some background information, and basic knowledge of the Microsoft Azure Machine Learning Studio environment will be covered. Finally, we will explore some practical applications to understand the amazing world of machine learning.

In this chapter, we will cover the following topics:

- Discovering the machine learning capabilities for classification, regression, clustering, and dimensionality reduction, including apps for automated model training and code generation
- A tour of the most popular machine learning algorithms to choose the right one for our needs
- Exploring the Azure Machine Learning Studio environment

By the end of this chapter, you will be able to recognize the different machine learning algorithms and the tools that Microsoft Azure Machine Learning Studio provides to handle them.

Machine learning overview

Machine learning is a multidisciplinary field created by intersection and synergy between computer science, statistics, neurobiology, and control theory. Its emergence has played a key role in several fields and has fundamentally changed the vision of software programming. If the question before was, *How can we program a computer?* now the question has become, *How will computers program themselves?*

Thus, it is clear that machine learning is a basic method that allows a computer to have its own intelligence.

Machine learning algorithms

The power of machine learning is due to the quality of its algorithms, which have been improved and updated over the years; these are divided into several main types depending on the nature of the signal used for learning or the type of feedback adopted by the system.

They are:

- **Supervised learning**: The algorithm generates a function that links input values to a desired output through the observation of a set of examples in which each data input has its relative output data; that is used to construct predictive models.
- **Unsupervised learning**: The algorithm tries to derive knowledge from a general input without the help of a set of pre-classified examples that are used to build descriptive models. A typical example of the application of these algorithms is search engines.
- **Reinforcement learning**: The algorithm is ability to learn depending on the changes that occur in the environment in which it is performed. In fact, since every action has some effect on the environment concerned, the algorithm is driven by the same feedback environment. Some of these algorithms are used in speech or text recognition.

Supervised learning

Supervised learning is a machine learning technique that aims to program a computer system so that it can resolve the relevant tasks automatically. To do this, the input data is included in a set *I* (typically vectors). Then the set of output data is fixed as set *O*, and finally it defines a function *f* that associates each input with the correct answer. Such information is called a **training set**.

These types of algorithms are based on learning by example theory: knowledge is gained by starting from a set of positive examples, which are instances of the concept to be learned, and negative examples, which are non-instances of the concept. In other words, there is a *teacher* who shows what is right and what is wrong; based on these teachings (training phase), the algorithm will learn to recognize new instances of the problem automatically, as shown in the following diagram:

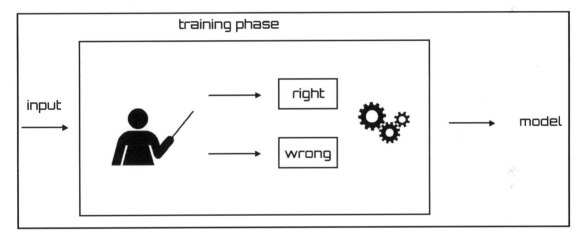

All supervised learning algorithms are based on the following thesis:

If an algorithm provides an adequate number of examples, it will be able to create a derived function B that will approximate the desired function A.

If the approximation of the desired function is adequate, when the input data is offered to the derived function, this function should be able to provide output responses similar to those provided by the desired function and then be acceptable. These algorithms are based on the "similar inputs correspond to similar outputs" concept.

Generally, in the real world, this assumption is not valid; however, some situations exist in which it is acceptable. Clearly, the proper functioning of such algorithms depends significantly on the input data. If there are only a few training inputs, the algorithm might not have enough experience to provide a correct output. Conversely, many inputs may make it excessively slow since the derivative function generated by a large number of inputs could be very complicated.

Moreover, experience shows that this type of algorithm is very sensitive to noise; even a few pieces of incorrect data can make the entire system unreliable and lead to wrong decisions. In supervised learning, it's possible to split problems based on the nature of the data. If the output value is categorical, such as membership/non-membership of a certain class, it is a classification problem. If the output is a continuous real value in a certain range, then it is a regression problem.

Unsupervised learning

The aim of unsupervised learning is to extract information from databases automatically. This process occurs without prior knowledge of the contents to be analyzed. Unlike supervised learning, there is no information on membership classes of the examples or generally on the output corresponding to a certain input. The goal is to get a model that is able to discover interesting properties, groups with similar characteristics (clustering) for instance, as shown in the following diagram:

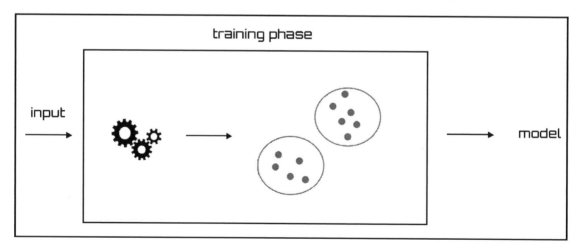

Search engines are an example of applications of these algorithms. Given one or more keywords, they are able to create a list of links related to our search.

The validity of these algorithms depends on the usefulness of the information they can extract from the databases. These algorithms work by comparing data and looking for similarities or differences. The available data concerns only the set of features that describe each example. They show great efficiency with elements of numeric type, but are much less accurate with non-numerical data. Generally, they work properly in the presence of data that contains an order or a clear grouping and is clearly identifiable.

Reinforcement learning

Reinforcement learning aims to create algorithms that can learn and adapt to environmental changes. This programming technique is based on the concept of receiving external stimuli depending on the algorithm choices. A correct choice will involve a premium, while an incorrect choice will lead to a penalty. The goal of the system is to achieve the best possible result, of course.

In supervised learning, there is a teacher that tells the system which is the correct output (learning with a teacher). This is not always possible. Often we have only qualitative information (sometimes binary, right/wrong, or success/failure).

The information available is called reinforcement signals. But the system does not give any information on how to update the agent's behavior (that is, weights). You cannot define a cost function or a gradient. The goal of the system is to create the smart agents that have a machinery able to learn from their experience, as shown in the following diagram:

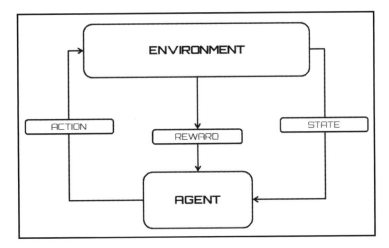

The agent (software) is a software entity that performs services on behalf of another program, usually automatically and invisibly.

Machine learning tasks

When we first venture into the use of artificial intelligence for data analysis, the first problem we are faced with is to choose the most appropriate algorithm for solving a specific problem. Analyzing the available algorithms, we immediately realize that the choice is not so immediate and requires an appropriate investigation.

A first approach to the problem involves the specification of the task that our machine learning algorithm will have to face. In this sense we can rest assured: there are only a handful of tasks to be analyzed even if, for each of these activities, different approaches and algorithms are available.

In fact, even if all machine learning algorithms take the same data as input, what they'll want to achieve is different. Machine learning algorithms can generally be classified into a few groups based on the tasks they were designed to solve. The typical activities in any automatic learning are as follows:

- Regression
- Classification
- Clustering
- Dimensionality reduction

In the following sections, we will analyze the characteristics using real-life examples.

Making predictions with regression algorithms

Since the dawn of time, human beings have tried to foresee the future. How many rainy days will there be in the next week? What will be the harvest for next season? These types of problems are regression problems. The goal is to predict the value of a continuous response variable. This is also a supervised learning task.

Regression analysis is a statistical process of studying the relationship between a set of independent variables (explanatory variables) and the dependent variable (response variable). Through this technique, it is possible to understand how the value of the response variable changes when the explanatory variable is varied.

Consider a group of bikes about which some information has been collected: number of years of use, number of kilometers traveled in one year, and number of falls. Through these techniques, we can find that on average, when the number of kilometers traveled increases, the number of falls also increases. By increasing the number of years of motorcycle usage and so increasing the experience, the number of falls tends to decrease.

A regression analysis can be conducted for dual purposes:

- **Explanatory**: To understand and weigh the effects of the independent variable on the dependent variable according to a particular theoretical model

- **Predictive**: To locate a linear combination of the independent variable so as to predict the value assumed by the dependent variable—optimally

To find the relationship between the variables, we can choose to describe the observation behavior by means of a mathematical function that, upon interpolating the data, can represent its tendency and keep its main information. The linear regression method consists of precisely identifying a line that is capable of representing point distribution in a two-dimensional plane. As it is easy to imagine, if the points corresponding to the observations are near the line, then the chosen model will be able to describe the link between the variables effectively.

In theory, there are an infinite number of lines that may interpolate the observations. In practice, there is only one mathematical model that optimizes the representation of the data. In the case of a linear mathematical relationship, the observations of the variable y can be obtained by a linear function of observations of the variable x. For each observation, we will have:

$$y = \alpha * x + \beta$$

In this formula, x is the explanatory variable and y is the response variable. Parameters α and β, which represent respectively the intercept with the y axis and the slope of the line, must be estimated based on the observations collected for the two variables included in the model. The following graph shows an example of a linear regression line.

The values of the ordinate can be predicted starting from those present on the abscissa with good approximation. In fact, all the observations are very close to the regression line:

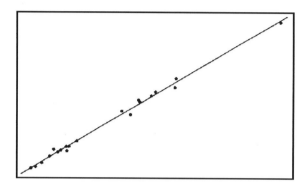

Of particular interest is the slope β, that is, the variation of the mean response for every single increment of the explanatory variable. What about a change in this coefficient? If the slope is positive, the regression line increases from left to right (as shown in the preceding graph); if the slope is negative, the line decreases from left to right. When the slope is zero, the explanatory variable has no effect on the value of the response. But it is not just the sign of β that establishes the weight of the relationship between the variables; more generally, its value is also important. In the case of a positive slope, the mean response is higher when the explanatory variable is higher; in the case of a negative slope, the mean response is lower when the explanatory variable is higher.

Regression techniques are workhorses of machine learning algorithms. The example of simple linear regression that we have just seen is the simplest case treated by this class of algorithms. Actually, much more complex problems can be faced with these techniques. This is due to the fact that the name regression refers to a large family of machine learning algorithms.

The most popular regression algorithms are:

- Ordinary least squares regression
- Linear regression
- Logistic regression
- Stepwise regression
- Multivariate adaptive regression splines

Each algorithm allows us to solve a specific class of problems; it is worth remembering that in any case, the goal is to predict the value of a continuous response variable.

Automated classification using machine learning

Classification algorithms study how to automatically learn to make accurate predictions based on observations. Starting from a set of predefined class labels, the algorithm gives each piece of data input a class label in accordance with the training model. If there are just two distinction classes, we talk about binary classification; otherwise, we go for multi-class classification. In more detail, each category corresponds to a different label; the algorithm attaches a label to each instance, which simply indicates which class the data belongs to. A procedure that can perform this function is commonly called a **classifier**. The following graph shows an automated classification of the Iris flower based on petal length and height, using discriminant analysis:

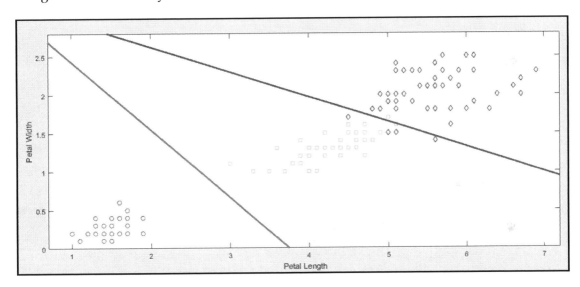

Classification has some analogy with regression: as well as regression, classification uses known labels of a training dataset to predict the response of the new dataset. The main difference between regression and classification is that regression is used to predict continuous values, whereas classification works with discrete data.

For example, regression can be used to predict the future price of oil based on its prices over the last 10 years. However, we should use the classification method to predict whether the price of oil will rise or decrease in the near future. In the first case, we use continuous data as a prediction and choose a continuous data response (the precise price of oil). In the second case, starting with continuous values (the price of oil over the last 10 years), we begin by classifying the various phases where a growth/diminution of price has been recorded; then we use that classification to predict a relative trend in the near future.

To approach a classification problem, several methods are available:

- Decision trees
- Naive Bayes algorithms
- Discriminant analysis
- K-nearest neighbors

Such algorithms provide appreciable performance when applied to problems with well-defined limits, where inputs follow a specific set of attributes and where the output has discrete values. The classification process takes advantage of the experience developed by evaluating new inputs through matching with previously observed and correctly labeled models.

A standard classification process includes the following steps:

1. **Training the algorithm**: In this step, the machine learning begins to work with the definition of the model and the next training. The model starts to extract knowledge from large amounts of data that we had available (training dataset); for this data, the couplings (instance or class) are available.
2. **Testing the algorithm**: In this step, we use the information learned in the previous step to see whether the model actually works. The evaluation of an algorithm is for seeing how well the model approximates the real system. In the case of supervised learning, we have some known values that we can use to evaluate the algorithm. If we are not satisfied, we can return to the previous steps, change some things, and retry the test.

Each classification algorithm, among those listed above, has its own peculiarities and is based on certain assumptions. We cannot say a priori which algorithm will provide us with the best performance. This is because the choice of the algorithm appropriate for our activity requires practice. In fact it is clear that no classifier will work best in all possible scenarios.

So, how will we choose the one that best fits our needs? To do this, simply compare the performance of different learning algorithms to select the best model for the specific problem; these may differ in the number of features or samples, the amount of noise in a dataset, and whether the classes are separable linearly or not. It will be enough to take the necessary patience and apply different algorithms before choosing the one that works best for our application.

Identifying groups using clustering methods

Clustering methods are designed to find hidden patterns or groupings in a dataset. Unlike the supervised learning methods covered in previous sections (regression and classification tasks), these algorithms identify a grouping without any label to learn from. They do so through the selection of clusters based on similarities between elements.

This is an unsupervised learning technique that groups statistical units to minimize the intra-group distance and maximize the inter-group distance. The distance between the groups is quantified by means of similarity/dissimilarity measures defined between the statistical units. In the following graph, four clusters are identified in a specific data distribution:

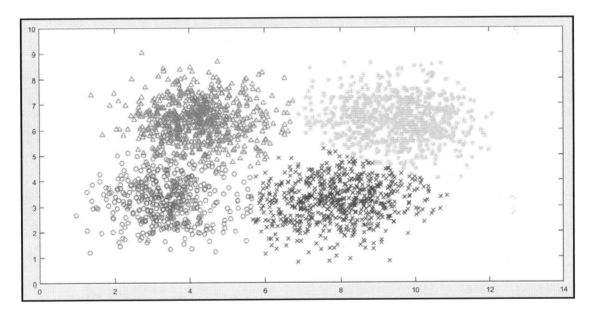

To perform cluster analysis, no prior interpretative model is required. In fact, unlike other multivariate statistical techniques, this one does not make an a priori assumption on the existing fundamental typologies that may characterize the observed sample. The cluster analysis technique has an exploratory role to look for existing but not-yet-identified structures in order to deduce the most likely group. This analysis is in fact a purely empirical method of classification, and as such, in the first place, it is an inductive technique.

In clustering, as in classification, we are interested in finding the law that allows us to assign observations to the correct class. But unlike classification, we also have to find a plausible subdivision of our classes.

While in classification we have some help from the target (the classification provided in the training set), in the case of clustering, we cannot rely on any additional information and we have to deduce the classes by studying the spatial distribution of data.

The areas where data is thickened correspond to similar observation groups. If we can identify observations that are similar to each other and at the same time different from those of another cluster, we can assume that these two clusters match different conditions. At this point, there are two things we need to go more deeply into:

- How to measure similarity?
- How to define a grouping?

The concept of distance and how to define a group are the two ingredients that describe a clustering algorithm. To approach a clustering problem, several methods are available; some of these are listed here:

- Hierarchical clustering
- K-means method
- K-medoids method
- Gaussian mixture models

Clustering involves identifying groupings of data. This is possible thanks to the measure of the proximity between the elements. The term proximity is used to refer to either similarity or dissimilarity. So, a group of data can be defined once you have chosen how to define the concept of similarity or dissimilarity. In many approaches, this proximity is conceived in terms of distance in a multidimensional space.

By the term similarity between two objects, we refer to the numerical measure of the degree to which the two objects are alike. On the contrary, by the term dissimilarity between two objects, we refer to the numerical measure of the degree to which two objects are unlike.

Similarities/dissimilarities between data objects can be measured by distance. Distances are dissimilarities with certain properties. For example, we can measure distance as Euclidean distance, but distance can be measured in so many other ways too. Some of them are listed here:

- Minkowski distance metric
- Manhattan distance metric
- Cosine distance metric

Once you have chosen a way to calculate the distance, you have to decide how to form groups. Two main algorithm families can be identified:

- **Hierarchical clustering works by creating a data hierarchy**: The data is described through a taxonomic tree, similar to those used in biology
- **Partitioning clustering works by making a data space partition**: The data space is divided into many subzones; the union of all the subzones gives full space, and one subzone is not superimposed onto other subzones

To summarize, in cluster analysis, we will try to maximize the similarity of intra-cluster (internal homogeneity) and to minimize the similarity of inter-cluster (external separation).

Dimensionality reduction to improve performance

When we handle large volumes of data, some issues occur spontaneously. How does one build a representative model of a set of hundreds of variables? How does one view data across countless dimensions? To address these issues, we must adopt a series of techniques called dimensionality reduction. Dimensionality reduction is the process of converting a set of data with many variables into data with lesser dimensions while ensuring similar information. The aim is to reduce the number of dimensions in a dataset through either feature selection or feature extraction without significant loss of details. Feature selection approaches try to find a subset of the original variables. Feature extraction reduces the dimensionality of the data by transforming it into new features.

Dimensionality reduction techniques are used to reduce two undesirable characteristics in data, namely noise (high variance values) and redundancy (highly correlated variables). These techniques help identify sets of unrelated predictive variables that can be used in subsequent analyses. Reducing a high-dimensional dataset, that is a dataset with many predictive variables, to one with fewer dimensions improves conceptualization. Preceding three dimensions, visualizing the data becomes difficult or impossible.

Feature selection

In general, when we work with high-dimensional datasets, it is a good idea to reduce the number of features to only the most useful ones and discard the rest. This can lead to simpler models that generalize better. Feature selection is the process of reducing inputs for processing and analyzing or identifying the most significant features over the others. This selection of features is necessary to create a functional model so as to achieve a reduction in cardinality, imposing a limit greater than the number of features that must be considered during its creation.

These methods help us identify and remove redundant and irrelevant and therefore unnecessary features. In fact, in building a predictive model, such features do not contribute to its accuracy; on the contrary, they can make it worse.

So, features should be used only if really useful and relevant:

- Fewer features imply more compact models that need fewer examples of learning to achieve good results
- Models that use fewer features are easier to understand for a human and more easily represented

Feature selection algorithms are essentially divided into three different classes:

- **Filter**: Select a subset of variables in the preprocessing phase, without taking into account the machine learning method that will be implemented later. Each new subset is used to train a model, which is tested on a new dataset. These methods are very computationally intensive, but they usually provide the best set of features for that particular model type.
- **Wrappers**: They use a specific machine learning model as a black box to determine the predictive power of a subset of variables. This method, however, requires an efficient research strategy and the cost depends on the method. This method then prepares what is a search of the sequential type (greedy methods) going to include/eliminate progressively new features according to their predictive capabilities.
- **Embedded**: Selection of variables as part of the training process, integrating features as variables of the discriminant function implemented in the machine learning method. The selection of the features is inserted in the optimization (training) of the predictive model. These approaches tend to be between filters and wrappers in terms of computational complexity.

Feature selection is particularly useful in cases where the modeling goal is to identify an influencing subset. It becomes essential when categorical features are present and numerical transformations are inadequate.

Feature extraction

When the data is too large to be processed, it is transformed into a reduced representation set of features. The process of transforming the input data into a set of features is called feature extraction. Indeed, feature extraction starts from an initial set of measured data and builds derivative values that can retain the information contained in the original dataset but emptied of redundant data.

The extraction of features means simplifying the cost of resources required to describe a large set of data accurately. When performing complex data analysis, one of the biggest problems is to limit the number of variables involved. An analysis of a large number of variables generally requires a large use of memory and processing or machine learning algorithms; they need a high adaptation threshold with test samples and they poorly generalize new samples. Features extraction is a general term for variable combination construction methods used to circumvent these problems but describe them with sufficient accuracy.

The most used feature extraction method is **principal component analysis (PCA)**. PCA generates a new set of variables, among them uncorrelated objects, called principal components; each main component is a linear combination of the original variables. All principal components are orthogonal to each other, so there is no redundant information. The principal components as a whole constitute an orthogonal basis for the data space. The goal of PCA is to explain the maximum amount of variance with the least number of principal components. PCA is a form of multidimensional scaling. It is a linear transformation of the variables into a lower dimensional space that retains the maximum amount of information about the variables. A principal component is therefore a combination of the original variables after a linear transformation.

In the following graph, you can see the results of PCA with the data distributed according to the first two principal components:

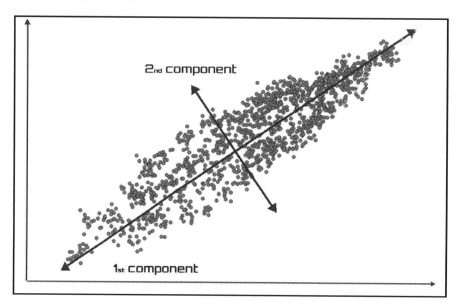

In this case, two new variables are represented, obtained as linear combinations of the original variables so that they are able to explain a significant portion of the total variance of the data. The method has a strong geometric connotation and has its theoretical justification in the theory of symmetric matrices.

The first main component explains the maximum percentage of the variability present in the data that can be represented in a single dimension. This component returns the direction along which maximum data dispersion is recorded. Furthermore, this percentage of explained variability can be calculated through the variance. The variance is in fact an index of the dispersion of data along a particular direction. Moreover, it is independent of the reference system: a rotation of the axes keeps the total variance in the data unchanged. The total variance is the sum of the variances along all the directions and a measure of the variability present in the dataset.

Azure Machine Learning Studio

Azure Machine Learning Studio is an interactive programming tool for machine learning analysis. This is the solution offered by Microsoft as a tool to create predictive models automatically without the need to know how the algorithm works. It is a platform in which data, cloud-based tools, and predictive analysis are combined to implement an effective model. The platform also has numerous APIs to help developers build advanced artificial intelligence models. Azure Machine Learning Studio is available at the following link: `https://studio.azureml.net/`.

The following screenshot shows the welcome page of Azure Machine Learning Studio:

In Azure Machine Learning Studio, building a development model becomes an interactive experience. It's more fun and much easier than the classic methodologies, which involve the implementation/adaptation of algorithms already available in libraries. In fact, thanks to the drag-and-drop function, it will be enough to select the necessary resources and the rest will be provided by Microsoft. Editing, saving a copy, running, converting, and publishing an experiment will be just as simple. All this is due to the visual connections available in the development environment, which does not require any programming experience, allowing in this way to develop models in a simple and fast manner.

In a time of shared experiences, a sharing place could not be missing even from Azure Machine Learning Studio. This is the Cortana Intelligence Gallery, where users can share and discover solutions among developers. The community also offers the possibility to interact with other developers in order to arrive at a shared solution of a specific problem.

Work sharing is not limited to the community offered by the Cortana Intelligence Gallery; in fact models designed in Azure Machine Learning Studio can be transferred directly to the web to get the best visibility possible. In this way, users can use our models and run them with their data. All the changes that will be made to the model will be updated in real time on the version available on the web.

Azure Machine Learning Studio account

In order to use the tools provided by the Azure Machine Learning Studio, you must first log in. No Azure subscription is required to access the environment. In fact, to create an Azure Machine Learning Studio account, we have two options:

- Choose anonymous guest access
- Sign in with our work, school, or Microsoft account

In addition, if we already have an Azure subscription, our Azure Machine Learning Studio account will automatically integrate with the Azure account.

Microsoft Azure Machine Learning Studio is another set of the Azure Cloud pay-for-play services. It is offered in two tiers—Free and Standard. In the following screenshot, features by tier are compared:

	FREE	STANDARD
Price	Free	$9.99 per seat per month $1 per studio experimentation hour
Azure subscription	Not required	Required
Max number of modules per experiment	100	Unlimited
Max experiment duration	1 hour per experiment	Up to 7 days per experiment with a maximum of 24 hours per module
Max storage space	10 GB	Unlimited - BYO
Read data from On-Premises SQL Preview	No	Yes
Execution/performance	Single node	Multiple nodes
Production Web API	No	Yes
SLA	No	Yes

To start exploring the contents of the environment we can, at least in the initial phase, use the services made available free of charge. Upgrade to the Standard version (paid) when our calculation needs will be passed to a professional level.

At the first access, a default workspace will be created, as shown in the following screenshot (Azure Machine Learning Studio dashboard):

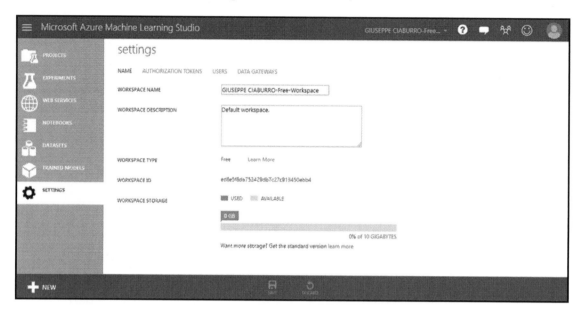

An Azure machine learning workspace contains all the tools you need to create, manage, and publish learning experiments on the cloud. On the left-hand bar, we can see the following features:

- **PROJECTS**: A list of projects created by us. Each project will contain a series of experiments, datasets, notebooks, and other resources.
- **EXPERIMENTS**: A list of all the experiments we have created. For each of them is summarized a series of characteristics—name, author, project, and so on.
- **WEB SERVICES**: Web services distributed by our experiments.
- **NOTEBOOKS**: The Jupyter notebooks we created. A Jupyter notebook is a document that contains live code, equations, visualizations, and explanatory text.
- **DATASETS**: A list of datasets we uploaded to studio.
- **TRAINED MODELS**: A list of models we have trained in our experiments and saved in the studio.
- **SETTINGS**: A collection of settings that you can use to configure your account and resources.

In the following sections, we will see how to use these tools to create a machine learning application.

Azure Machine Learning Studio experiment

The Azure Machine Learning Studio activities are called experiments. An experiment consists of datasets that provide data to analytical modules, which are linked together to build a machine learning model.

The following are the essential steps of a project:

1. Get the data
2. Prepare the data
3. Train the model
4. Score and evaluate the model
5. Use the model

To create a new experiment, just click on the + button at the bottom-left and a pop-up window will open, providing the following options:

- Blank experiment
- Experiment tutorial
- Some sample experiment

The following screenshot shows an overview of the pop-up window opened:

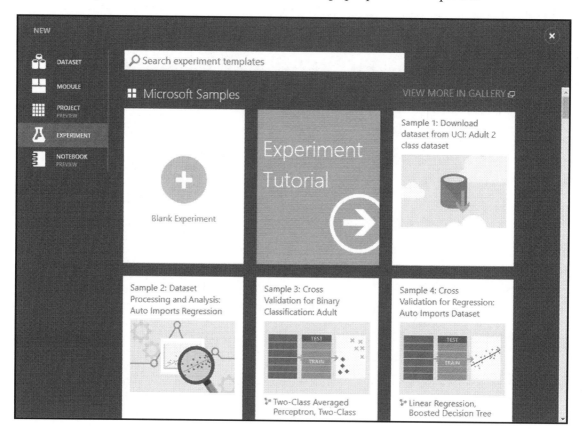

The essential elements of an experiment are:

- Dataset
- Module

Let's describe them in detail

Dataset

A dataset includes the data loaded in Azure Machine Learning Studio to be used in the modeling process. In the Azure Machine Learning Studio, some sample datasets are included to try using the program. You can load other datasets using one of the following options:

- Load data from a local file on the hard disk of the machine you are using to create a dataset in the workspace
- Access data from one of the different online data sources while the experiment runs through the import data module
- Use data from another experiment saved as a dataset
- Use data from a local SQL Server database

When an experiment is set up, you can choose a dataset from those available on the left-hand side of the work area.

Module

A module is an algorithm that can be applied to data. A large number of machine learning algorithms are available in Azure Machine Learning Studio. But the development environment is not limited to this by providing numerous tools for preparing and displaying data. Using these components, it is possible to develop an experiment of machine learning analysis to run the iteration on it and to use it to perform the training of the model. The model obtained can thus be saved in the Azure Cloud so that it can be used to obtain new data.

The algorithms present in the studio allow us to face the following machine learning tasks:

- Clustering
- Anomaly detection
- Regression
- Two-class classification
- Multi-class classification
- Computer vision
- Text analytics
- Statistical functions

When an experiment is set up, you can choose a module from those available on the left-hand side of the work area (**module palette**).

Work area

As we said before, when the + button is clicked on, a pop-up window is opened. If we choose a blank experiment option, a work area is opened, as shown in the following screenshot:

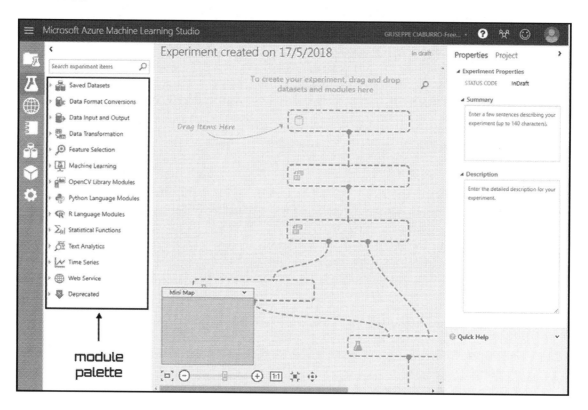

Blank experiment template

As shown in the screenshot, to create an experiment, it will be enough to drag and drop a dataset and modules into the flowchart that appears in the center of the work area. Items to be added to the workflow can be retrieved using the column menu (**module palette**) that appears to the left of the window. All that we need is located in this window: to understand how to use the tools available we will see a practical example in the next section.

At the bottom of the canvas, a useful bar is present, as shown in the following screenshot:

Using this bar, it is possible to save and run an experiment, among other things. In this section, we presented the graphical interface of Azure Machine Learning Studio. In the next section, we will see how it works using a practical example.

Breast cancer detection

The breast is made up of a set of glands and adipose tissue, and is placed between the skin and the chest wall. In fact, it is not a single gland but a set of glandular structures, called lobules, joined together to form a lobe. In a breast, there are 15 to 20 lobes. The milk reaches the nipple from the lobules through small tubes called milk ducts.

Breast cancer is a potentially serious disease if it is not detected and treated for a long time. It is caused by uncontrolled multiplication of some cells in the mammary gland that are transformed into malignant cells. This means that they have the ability to detach themselves from the tissue that has generated them to invade the surrounding tissues and eventually other organs of the body. In theory, cancers can be formed from all types of breast tissues, but the most common ones are from glandular cells or from those forming the walls of the ducts.

The objective of this example is to identify each of a number of benign or malignant classes. To do this, we will use the data contained in the dataset named Breast Cancer (Wisconsin Breast Cancer database). This data has been taken from databases in the UCI Machine Learning Repository; DNA samples arrive periodically as Dr. Wolberg reports his clinical cases. The database therefore reflects this chronological grouping of the data. This grouping information appears immediately, having been removed from the data itself. Each variable except the first was converted into 11 primitive numerical attributes, with values ranging from 0 through 10.

To get the data, we draw on the large collection of data available in the UCI Machine Learning Repository at: http://archive.ics.uci.edu/ml.

The data frames contain 699 observations on 11 variables:

- `Id`: Sample code number
- `Cl.thickness`: Clump thickness
- `Cell.size`: Uniformity of cell size
- `Cell.shape`: Uniformity of cell shape
- `Marg.adhesion`: Marginal adhesion
- `Epith.c.size`: Single epithelial cell size
- `Bare.nuclei`: Bare nuclei
- `Bl.cromatin`: Bland chromatin
- `Normal.nucleoli`: Normal nucleoli
- `Mitoses`: Mitoses
- `Class`: Class (0 = benign, 1 = malignant)

As we said before, the essential steps of a project are listed here:

1. Get the data
2. Prepare the data
3. Train the model
4. Score and evaluate the model

So the first thing to do is recover the data.

Get the data

As the data source, we will use the dataset downloaded from the UCI Machine Learning Repository. These are now available on our PC in `.csv` format. The first operation to be performed will be uploading the dataset to the Azure Machine Learning Studio. To do this, we will perform the following steps:

1. Click on **+ NEW** at the bottom of the Azure Machine Learning workspace window.
2. Select **DATASET**.
3. Select **FROM LOCAL FILE**. The following window is opened:

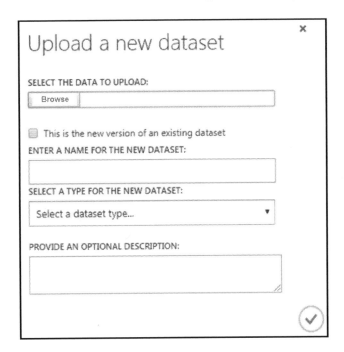

4. In the **Upload a new dataset** dialog window, click on **Browse** and find the `.csv` file in the local filesystem.
5. Enter a name for the dataset or accept the proposed name.
6. For data type, select **Generic CSV File** with header (`.csv`).
7. Add a description if you like.
8. Click on the OK check mark.

After uploading the data, a new dataset appears in the dataset window. This dataset is now available for any kind of analysis. Now that the data is loaded into the workspace, we can include it in our experiment. To do this, we create a new experiment:

1. Just click on the **+** button at the bottom left of the Azure Machine Learning Studio workspace and a pop-up window will open.
2. Choose a blank experiment option and an experiment canvas is opened
3. In the module palette to the left of the experiment canvas, expand **Saved Datasets**
4. Under **My Datasets**, drag `.csv` onto the canvas

The following screenshot shows a new dataset module added onto the experiment canvas:

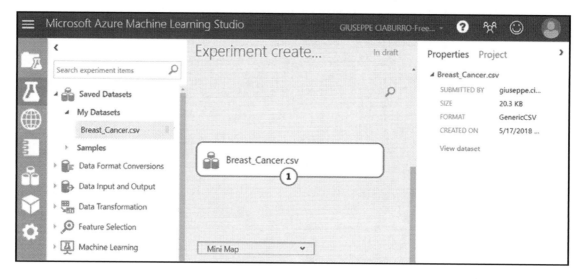

To get a data overview and some statistical information, right-click on the output port of the dataset (the small circle at the bottom with number **1**) and select **Visualize**. A new window is opened, with a summary of the contents of the file (numbers of rows and columns). Furthermore, all the columns of the dataset are available. For each one, the name, a histogram of the data, and the values relative to the first lines are given. To get more statistics, just click on the column that interests you. In this way, on the right-hand side of the window will be reported a series of statistics: **Mean, Median, Min, Max, Standard Deviation, Unique Values, Missing Values**, and **Feature Type**. Furthermore, you can view the histogram of the data contained in this column as shown in the following screenshot:

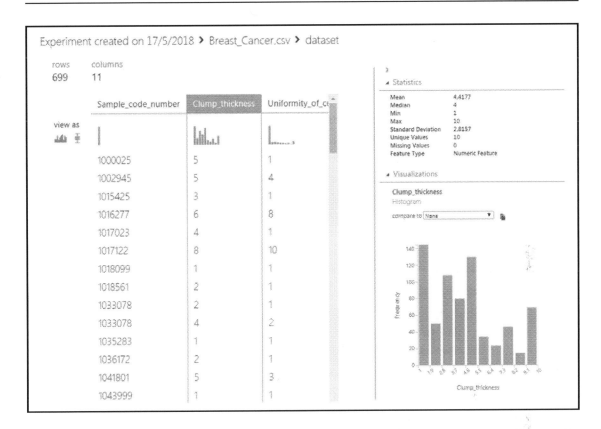

All modules in the canvas will be equipped with ports (input/output) represented by small circles: the input ports at the top and the output ports at the bottom. Previously, we used the output port of the dataset to get a view. By connecting one module's output port to the input port of another, it is possible to create a data stream in the experiment. To preview the data status at a specific point, simply click on the output port of a dataset or module. Through this analysis, we can notice if some column contains a missing value.

Prepare the data

After having imported the data, it is necessary to prepare it appropriately before executing any type of analysis (preprocessing). In fact, often in loading data, it may happen that some values are omitted (by mistake or because there are no observations). Any absence of values in columns and rows can distort the whole analysis. For this reason, it is necessary to clean up these missing values.

A missing value occurs when an unknown value is stored for the variable in an observation. Missing data is a common occurrence and can have a significant effect on the operations that can be done on the data.

The following are some of the main tasks in data preprocessing:

- **Data cleaning**: Filling missing values; detecting and removing noisy data and outliers
- **Data reduction**: Reduction of the number of attributes for easier data management
- **Data discretization**: Converting continuous attributes into categorical attributes
- **Data transformation**: Normalizing the data to reduce size and noise
- **Cleaning text**: Removing embedded characters that can cause data misalignments

Now we will just delete the missing values in the dataset. To do this, we will use the **Clean Missing Data** module in Azure Machine Learning Studio. It should be noted that the cleaning method used can have a significant influence on the results as well as the presence of missing data. Experimenting with different methods can help us to identify the best method that eliminates this problem by preserving the characteristics of the data.

To start, we add the **Clean Missing Data** module to the experiment and connect the dataset with missing values. The **Clean Missing Data** module is contained in the **Data Transformation | Manipulation** path. Remember that to connect two modules, you just have to click on the output port of a module, keep it clicked, and connect it to the input port of another module. Then select the **Clean Missing Data** module. At the right of the canvas in the **Properties** tab, set the properties of this operation, as shown in the following screenshot:

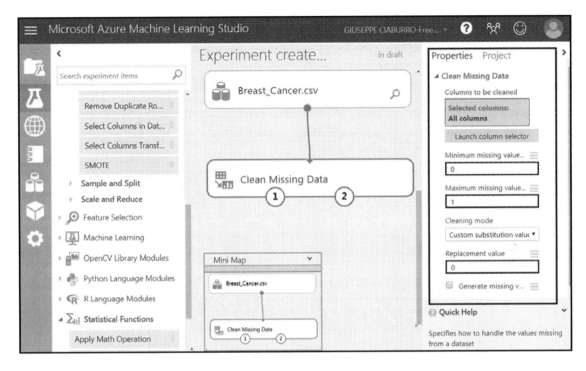

By default, the **Clean Missing Data** module applies cleaning to all columns. Therefore, if you need to clean several columns using different methods, use separate instances of the form. To select different columns, we can use the column selector.

Then two boxes are present: **Minimum missing value ratio** and **Maximum missing value ratio**. In these boxes, we can specify the minimum and maximum numbers of missing values that can be present for the operation to be performed. By default, the **Minimum missing value ratio** property is set to 0. This means that missing values are cleaned even if there is only one missing value. By default, the **Maximum missing value ratio** is set to 1. This means that missing values are cleaned even if 100% of the values in the column are missing.

After these, the **Cleaning mode** property is available: In this drop-down menu, we can select options for replacing or removing missing values. The following options are available:

- **Replace using MICE**
- **Custom substitution value**
- **Replace with mean**

- **Replace with median**
- **Replace with mode**
- **Remove entire row**
- **Remove entire column**
- **Replace using Probabilistic PCA**

In our case, having a very large number of observations (699), we decide to delete the entire row (**Remove entire row**) wherever there is a missing value.

After correctly setting the cleaning operations, we can launch the procedure by just clicking on the **Run** button at the bottom of the canvas.

Train the model

This is the most important phase; in fact it is time to build and train our machine learning model. In this step, the machine learning begins to work with the definition of the model and the next training. The model starts to extract knowledge from the large amounts of data that we had available, and nothing has been explained so far.

Let's now split the data for the training and the test model. Training and testing the model forms the basis for further usage of the model in predictive analytics. Given a dataset of 699 rows of data, which includes the predictor and response variables, we split the dataset into a convenient ratio (say 70:30) and allocate 490 rows for training and 209 rows for testing. The rows are selected at random to reduce bias. Once the training data is available, the data is fed to the machine learning algorithm to get the massive universal function in place. The training data determines the features to be used to get to the output from the input.

Once sufficient convergence is achieved, the model is stored in memory and the next step is to test the model. We pass the 209 rows of data to check whether the actual output matches with the predicted output from the model. Testing is done to get various metrics that can validate the model. If the accuracy is too wary, the model has to be rebuilt with changes in the training data and other parameters passed to the machine learning algorithm.

As anticipated, the training and test of the model will be performed with separate data in a dataset for the training and in another dataset for the testing phase. To split the dataset into two subdivisions of appropriately divided data, we will use the **Split Data** module. To do this, we will run the following procedure:

1. To start, select and drag the **Split Data** module into the canvas area; connect it to the output of the **Clean Missing Data** module. This is the last module inserted in the flowchart.

2. Click on the **Split Data** module and select it. The **Split Data** module is located in the following path of the left-hand sidebar: **Data Transformation | Sample and Split**. Find the **Fraction of rows in the first output dataset** option in the **Properties** panel to the right of the canvas and set it to 0.7. In this way, 70% of the data will be used to perform the model training and 30% for the model testing. It is clear that in order to identify the model that best approximates our data, it is possible to experiment with different percentages.

In the following screenshot the essential elements of the last procedure analyzed are shown:

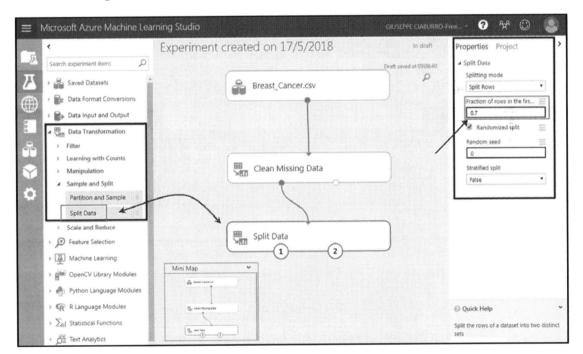

As we can see in the preceding screenshot, the **Split Data** module has two output ports: **1** is the training set, **2** is the testing set. We can also note that in the canvas **Properties** section, the **Randomized split** parameter is set. This means that 70% of the data is output through the first port of the module randomly; so the first 490 rows are not taken in succession, but that number of lines is randomly taken over the entire dataset. Obviously, this procedure is also used for the testing dataset. Furthermore, the **Random seed** parameter is also present, which controls the seeding of the pseudo random number generator. All this to make the example we are going to make reproducible.

At this point, we have the two datasets for training and testing. The time has come to choose the machine learning algorithm. As we said at the beginning of the section, the problem we want to tackle is to recognize the type of breast cancer based on some measured parameters. Obviously, this is a classification problem. The output variable (Output_Class) takes only two values (0, 1), which correspond to the two diagnoses (benign, malignant).

One way to address a classification problem is to use logistic regression. Logistic regression is a methodology used to predict the value of a dichotomous dependent variable on the basis of a set of explanatory variables, both qualitative and quantitative. The dependent variable is a qualitative response of dichotomous type, and it describes the outcome or success concerning the occurrence of a random event. Follow this procedure:

1. To select the learning algorithm, expand the **Machine Learning** category in the module palette to the left of the canvas area, and then expand **Initialize Model**. You will see different categories of modules that can be used to initialize machine learning algorithms. For this experiment, select the **Two-Class Logistic Regression** module from the **Classification** category and drag it into the experiment canvas area.

2. Once the machine learning algorithm has been chosen, it is necessary to add the module that allows us to train the model: **Train Model**. This module allows us to train a model after having defined and set its parameters and requires tagged data. You can also use **Train Model** to redevelop an existing model with new data. The **Train Model** module is located in the following path of the module palette: **Machine Learning | Train**. Drag the **Train Model** module to the experiment canvas area.

3. Connect the output port of the **Two-Class Logistic Regression** module to the left input port of the **Train Model** module and connect the left data output port of the **Split Data** module to the right input port of the **Train Model** module.

4. At this point, a symbol in the box relating to the **Train** module reminds us that something needs to be set. Click on the **Train Model** module. Click on the **Launch column selector** in the **Properties** pane to the right of the canvas, and then select the Output_Class column. This is the value that we intend to estimate with the model.

In the following screenshot are highlighted the essential elements used in the previous procedure:

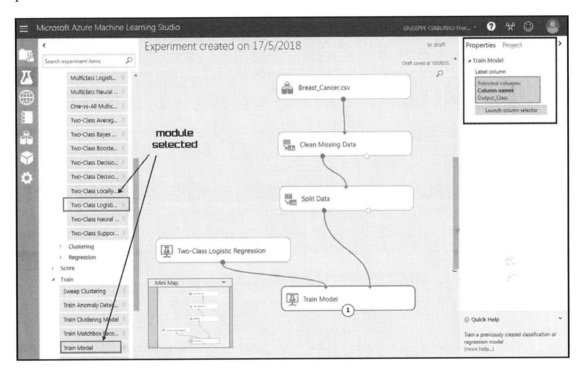

At this point it is possible to run the experiment. The result is a logistic regression model the training of which was performed. It can be used to assign a class to the new data related to the clinical tests carried out on people in order to detect the nature of cancer formation (benign, malignant).

Score and evaluate the model

As we anticipated in the previous section, so far we have used 70% of the data for model training; now it is possible to use the remaining 30% to test its functioning. To do this, we will use the **Score Model** module. This module scores predictions for a trained classification or regression model. Follow this procedure:

1. Select the **Score Model** module. The **Score Model** module is located at the following path of the module palette: **Machine Learning | Score**. Drag the **Score Model** module to the experiment canvas area.
2. Connect the output port of the **Train Model** module to the left input port of the **Score Model** module.
3. Connect the test data output port of the **Split Data** module (right output port) to the right input port of the **Score Model**.
4. Run the experiment.

In the following screenshot, the essential elements used in the previous procedure are highlighted:

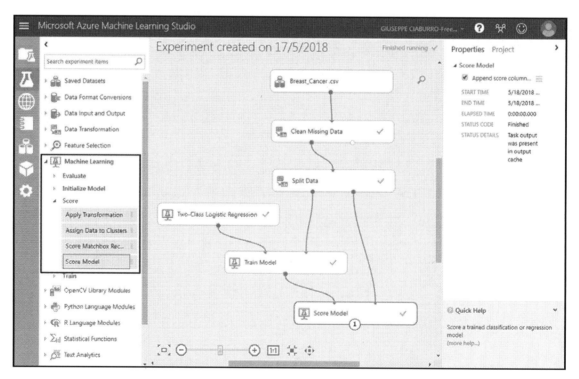

To analyze the test simulation results, just right-click on the output port of **Score Model** and select **Visualize**. The output shows the estimated values for breast cancer and the values known from the test data, as shown in the following screenshot:

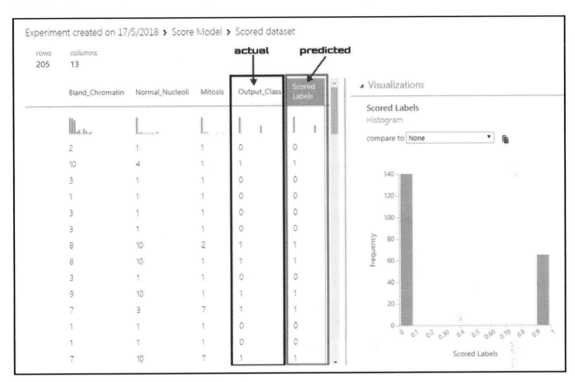

From the analysis of the screenshot, it is possible to notice that the forecast seems to have provided good results. But let's try to evaluate the results obtained more rigorously. To evaluate the quality of the results, we can use the **Evaluate Model** module. This module evaluates the results of a classification or regression model with standard metrics. Follow this procedure now:

1. Select the **Evaluate Model** module. The **Evaluate Model** module is located at the following path of the module palette: **Machine Learning | Evaluate**. Drag the **Score Model** module into the experiment canvas area.

2. Connect the output port of the **Score Model** module to the left input port of the **Evaluate Model** module.

3. Run the experiment.

To view the **Evaluate Model** output, right-click on the output port and select **Visualize**. The following metrics are reported:

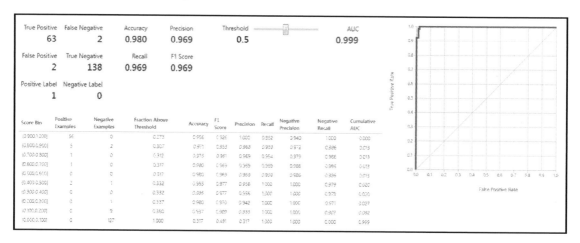

In the preceding screenshot, the terms are defined as follows:

- **True Positive (TP)**: All cases where the predicted and actual values are both true (1 = malignant).
- **True Negative (TN)**: All cases where the predicted value is false and the actual value is also false (0 = benign).
- **False Positive (FP)**: This is a case where we predict something as positive (true), but it is actually negative.
- **False Negative (FN)**: Where we predict something as false, but actually it is true.
- **Accuracy**: This is the measure of how good our model is. It is expected to be closer to 1 if our model is performing well.
- **Precision and Recall**: These are again ratios between the TP with (TP + FP) and TP with (TP + FN) respectively. These ratios determine how relevant our predictions are compared to the actual values.
- **F1 Score**: This is computed as the weighted average of precision and recall between 0 and 1, where the ideal F1 score value is 1.
- **AUC**: This measures the area under the curve plotted with true positives on the y axis and false positives on the x axis.

It should be noted that our model is able to adapt very well to the data. In fact, the evaluation of the model provided an accuracy value equal to 0.98.

Summary

In this chapter, we introduced the basic concepts of machine learning and the different types of algorithm. We explored different types of machine learning algorithms depending on the nature of the signal used for learning or the type of feedback adopted by the system. Then, typical activities in any automatic learning were covered: regression, classification, clustering, and dimensionality reduction. In addition, an introduction, some background information, and basic knowledge of Microsoft Azure Machine Learning Studio environment were covered. Finally, we explored a practical application to understand the amazing world of machine learning.

6
Introduction to Azure Databricks

So far in this book, we have seen that ETL can be done on-premises with an existing SSIS implementation. For cloud ETL, we used **Azure Data Lake Analytics (ADLA)**. Sparks is one of the other major players when it comes to data integration on the cloud. Databricks is Sparks' latest addition in Azure services at the time of writing this book. It is meant to be simple to set up and use while delivering fast performance in a production environment.

In this chapter, we'll see how ADF can trigger a Databricks notebook run. Later in this book, we'll show how we can integrate this data into a Power BI report. This chapter introduces only the simple Databricks integration in ADF.

Azure Databricks setup

This section describes how to set up Databricks in Azure. Once logged in to the Azure portal, click on **Create a resource** in the top-left corner and select the **Analytics** category. As shown in the following screenshot, click on **Azure Databricks**:

We're now redirected to the **Azure Databricks Service** blade. We first need to set up a workspace, as shown in the following screenshot:

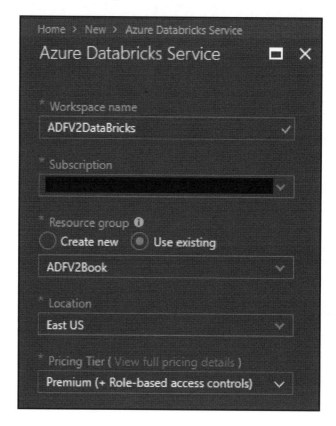

The parameters are explained here:

- **Workspace name**: `ADFV2DataBricks`
- **Subscription**: The subscription in use when you logged in to Azure
- **Resource group**: The same as we have used since the beginning—`ADFV2Book`
- **Location**: The same location of all our resources used so far
- **Pricing Tier**: **Premium**. This is mandatory to be able to connect Power BI to Databricks

Once done, check the **Pin to dashboard** option and click on **Create** at the bottom-left of the blade to create the workspace. After a few minutes, the workspace is ready to use, as shown in this screenshot:

A workspace is a placeholder or folder where we store all our assets, such as notebooks, libraries, and so on. Clicking on the Databricks workspace tile brings us to its blade, as shown in the following screenshot:

We'll now click on **Launch Workspace** to log in to Databricks and get to the Azure Databricks landing page. As shown in the following screenshot, the **Clusters** icon is highlighted. This is where we'll continue our journey to Azure Databricks setup:

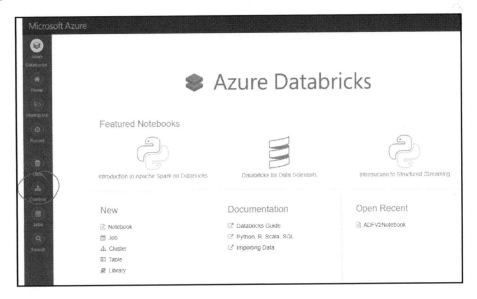

Click on **Clusters** to get into the **Clusters** section. Clusters are the computing resource used by our notebooks to interact and transform the data.

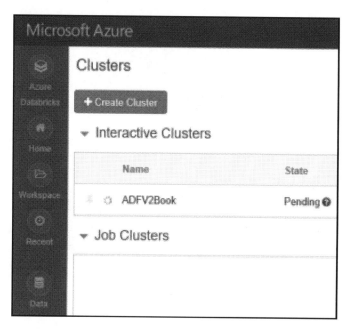

There are two types of clusters:

- **Interactive Clusters**: These are the clusters we use to design our notebooks and interact with the data. These clusters are also used by Power BI or other reporting tools to retrieve our analysis and create reports.
- **Job Clusters**: These clusters are used by ADF to run notebooks. We'll use them later in this chapter.

Since we're just beginning with our workspace and do not have any notebook created yet, we're now going to create an interactive cluster. Clicking on **Create Cluster** will bring us to the cluster creation window, as shown in the following screenshot:

Leave all options as they are. Simply use **Standard** as the **Cluster Type** since this is the cluster used by ADF.

Next, we're going to create a folder to store our notebook. As shown in the following screenshot, click on the **Workspace** icon; then select the arrow at the top and choose **Create | Folder** from the submenu:

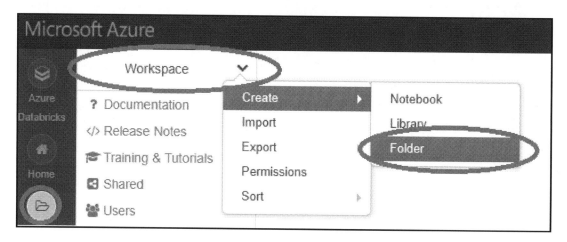

Name the folder ADFCalls. We'll create our notebook inside of it.

Prepare the data to ingest

Now that we've created our cluster and folder, we must prepare some data to work with. For this book, we're using the data warehouse data available in the on-premise SQL database we created in the first chapters. This will allow us to see another integration runtime: self-hosted. We'll copy the data in the Azure storage account created previously in this chapter.

Setting up the folder in the Azure storage account

Going back to the Azure portal, we'll create a blob container and call it sales-data, as shown in the following screenshot:

Enter a valid name: `sales-data`. Click on **OK** when done. This creates the container in the `adfv2book` blob storage account, as shown in this screenshot:

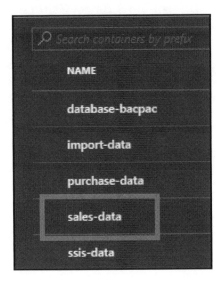

Now that the container is ready, let's go back to the factory to prepare the self-hosted runtime.

Self-hosted integration runtime

A self-hosted integration runtime is necessary when we want to access data in the on-premise Windows machine from ADF. This is a secure tunnel that allows ADF to read or write data to a database or files. This section will describe how to set up this tunnel.

1. Going back to the factory, we select the **Connections** section and then select **Integration Runtimes**, as shown in the following screenshot. Click on **+ New**:

2. This brings forth the **Integration Runtime Setup** wizard. Select the first integration runtime and click on **Next.**

3. We discussed earlier in this book the two types of self-hosted integration runtime; one is for a public (cloud) network, like the default runtime available with ADF by default. The other one is used to access private networks and machines, exactly what we want to do here. We'll use the **Private Network** integration runtime. Click on **Next**. The last step is used to name our integration runtime; name it WWImportersDW and click on **Next**.

4. The final step is to download and set up an integration runtime service. This is a Windows service that will allow communication or a tunnel between your PC and ADF. As shown in the following screenshot, we have two options. **Express setup** will install the integration runtime on your local machine and set up the authentication keys to create the communication service.

Integration Runtime Setup   ✕

Install integration runtime on Windows machine or add further nodes using the Authentication Key.

◢ **Integration Runtime Settings**

Option 1: Express setup

Click here to launch the express setup for this computer

Option 2: Manual setup

Step 1: Download and install integration runtime

Step 2: Use this key to register your integration runtime

The second option requires us to download the ADF integration runtime. It directs you to the following URL: `https://www.microsoft.com/en-us/download/details.aspx?id=39717`. Click on **Download** to continue.

5. You will be asked to choose the download. Check the first option and click on **Next.**
6. Once downloaded, start the installation of the executable. Choose the language you want and click on **Next** to continue.
7. Read and accept the terms and conditions. Click on **Next.**
8. Choose the destination folder and click on **Next.**
9. Finally, click on **Install** to proceed with the installation.

10. If you're using a laptop, you will get this message when the installation completes. It simply tells you that the service will not be available if your PC goes to sleep or hibernates. Click on **OK** to dismiss it:

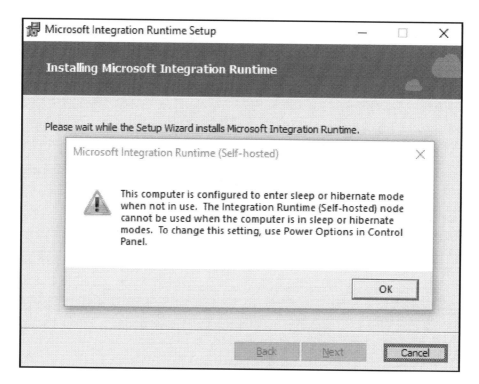

 In a real-world scenario, we wouldn't use a laptop to install the integration runtime. It would be installed on a machine that is not going to sleep or hibernate. Usually, we use a small server that has access to the data sources. We should never install it on a laptop or a database server.

11. Once we've clicked on **Finish** in the last step of the wizard, a window opens and asks us for the authentication key, as shown in the following screenshot:

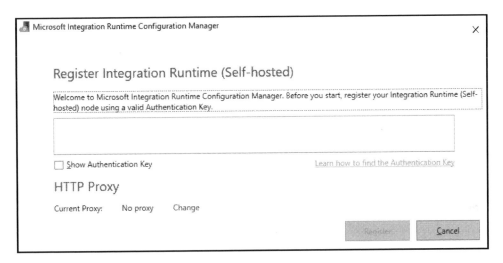

12. This key is found on the **Integration Runtime Setup**. Go back to the factory; if you've followed the steps in this section, you should have a step like the one in this screenshot:

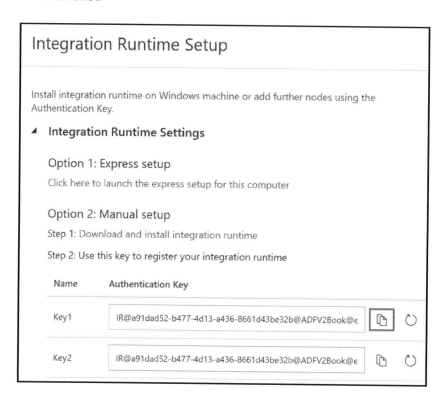

13. Click on the copy icon as highlighted. You will get a confirmation message that the content has been copied to your local clipboard.

14. Go back to the **Microsoft Integration Runtime Configuration Manager** and paste the authentication key content; you should see a screen like this:

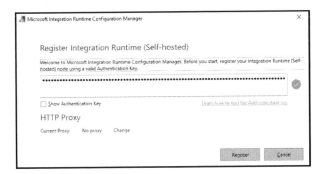

15. Click on **Register** to link the integration runtime with your ADF. In ADF, click on **Finish** to complete the integration runtime setup in the factory. You should see the newly created integration runtime in the list, as shown in the following screenshot:

Linked service setup

Now that we have created the integration runtime and linked it to our local PC, we're going to create a linked service that will use it in ADF.

1. On the **Connections** tab, select **Linked Services** and click on **+ New**. The **New Linked Service** blade appears. Select **SQL Server** in the **Data Store** section and click on **Continue**:

2. The next step asks us for a name; we'll use WWImportersDWADFV2Book. Add a description if necessary. Set the properties as shown in this screenshot:

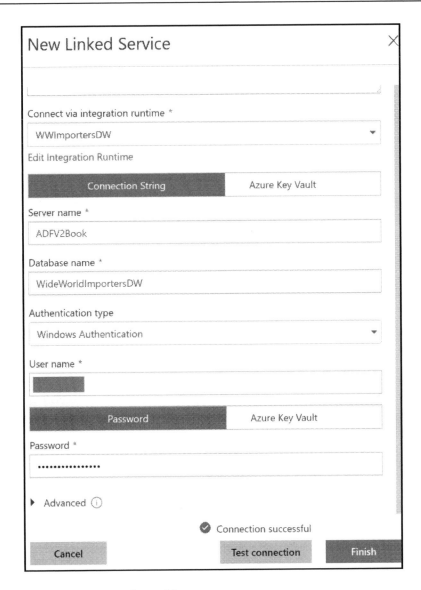

The properties are explained here:

- **Connect via integration runtime**: Choose WWImportersDW, the self-hosted integration runtime we created earlier in this chapter.
- **Connection String**: We're using a **Connection String** to connect to the database.
- **Server name**: The SQL Server name; in our case, we used ADFV2Book. Yours might be different.

- **Database name**: WideWorldImportersDW.
- **Authentication type: Windows Authentication.**
- **User name**: Your Windows username to connect to the SQL Server.
- **Password**: Your Windows password.

3. Click on the **Test connection** to make sure you're able to connect to your on-premise server from ADF. When your connection is successful, click on **Finish** to complete the linked service. The newly created linked service should appear in the list as shown in the following screenshot:

Datasets setup

Now that we have set up our linked service, we 're going to create two datasets: one to copy data from SQL Server and the other to write into our sales-data container.

SQL Server dataset

We're going to copy some data from our on-premise SQL Server. To create the dataset, we need to create a structure in SQL Server that will be available in ADF. In our case, we'll use an SQL view.

Here is the view code. Execute it on your local SQL Server in SSMS; we'll use it later in the dataset:

```
CREATE SCHEMA ADFV2Book;
GO
CREATE VIEW ADFV2Book.Sales AS
SELECT          dt.Date, Cust.Customer, Sales.Package, Sales.Description,
SUM(Sales.Quantity) AS Quantity, SUM(Sales.[Unit Price]) AS [Unit Price],
AVG(Sales.[Tax Rate]) AS [Tax Rate], SUM(Sales.[Total Excluding Tax])
                    AS [Total Excluding Tax], AVG(Sales.[Tax Amount])
AS [Tax Amount], AVG(Sales.Profit) AS Profit, SUM(Sales.[Total Including
Tax]) AS [Total Including Tax]
FROM            Fact.Sale AS Sales INNER JOIN
                    Dimension.Customer AS Cust ON Sales.[Customer Key]
= Cust.[Customer Key] INNER JOIN
                    Dimension.Date AS dt ON Sales.[Invoice Date Key] =
dt.Date
```

```
GROUP BY dt.Date, Cust.Customer, Sales.Package, Sales.Description;
GO
```

We first create a schema: `ADFV2Book`. This schema will hold the view `Sales` created thereafter. Going back to our factory, we'll now create a dataset. From the pipeline section, click on the + sign and choose **Dataset** from the menu that appears, as shown in the following screenshot:

We'll name the dataset `ADFV2Book_Sales`. Click on the **Connection** tab. Set the properties as shown in the following screenshot. Once done, click on **Preview data**. A window pops up and you can see the first few lines of the view content:

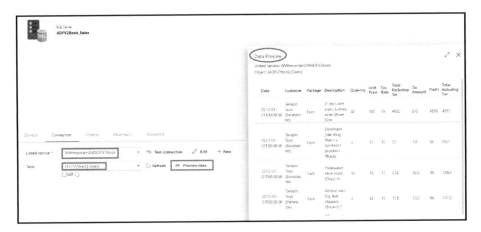

The previous step proved that ADF can access your local server from the cloud.

Blob storage dataset

Linked service

The blob storage linked service is much easier to create as we're not using the default integration runtime that came with the factory. Go to the **Connections** and create a new linked service. Choose **Azure Blob Storage** from the **Data Store** tab as shown in the following screenshot and click on **Continue**:

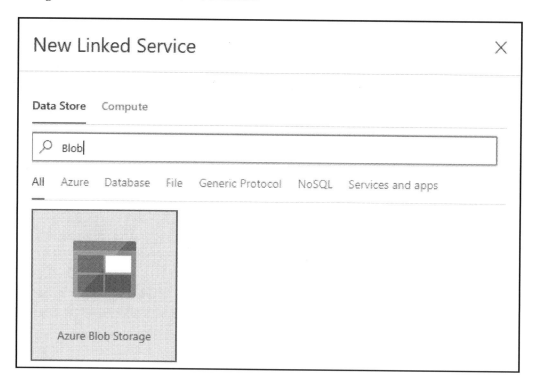

Name it `Blob_AzureV2Book_Sales` and adjust the other properties as shown in the following screenshot. Click on **Test connection** to make sure that everything works properly, and click on **Finish** when done. That's it! We created the linked service in one step, much simpler than the one on SQL Server on-premise.

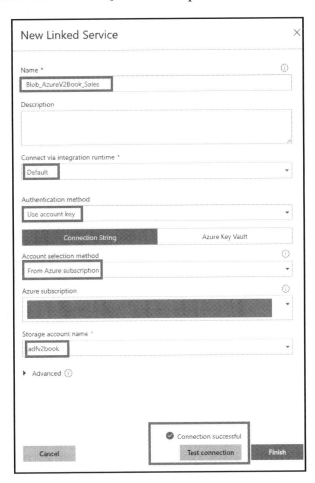

Dataset

Add a new dataset and name it `ADFV2Book_Sales_Destination`, as shown in the following screenshot:

Click on **Connection** to go to the connection information's tab. Set the properties as shown in the following screenshot:

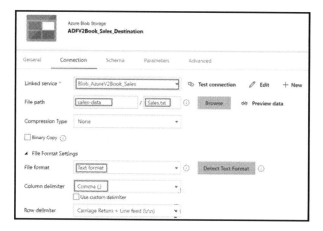

Now that the dataset is completed, click on **Publish All** at the top of the factory to save your work to the ADF service, as shown in this screenshot:

Copy data from SQL Server to sales-data

All the steps we took in the previous section were preparing the copy activity we're going to do in this section. What we have done manually so far is essentially take the same steps that the copy activity wizard would have done. Since we're now more familiar with ADF, it's good to do it manually to better understand all the steps of a copy activity process.

We'll now add a new pipeline to our factory. We could work from the one we created to hold our Execute SSIS package activity, but since we want to test and debug the new code, it's easier to use another pipeline. If we don't do it, we would have to execute all the pipeline every time we want to test a single activity. Once we are satisfied with our work, we will copy/paste it back into the main pipeline.

Drag a **Copy** activity from the **Dataflow** section of the activities. Name it `Copy_ADFFV2Book_Sales_Blob`, as shown in the following screenshot:

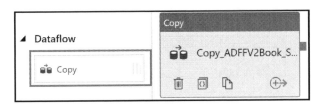

Click on the **Source** tab and, using the drop-down list, select the `ADFV2Boook_Sales_Source` in the **Source Dataset,** as shown in the following screenshot. This is the dataset that is linked to the `ADFV2Book.Sales` view in SQL Server on-premise:

Click on the **Sink** tab and select `ADFV2Book_Sales_Destination` as the **Sink Dataset**. Your screen should look like this screenshot:

Now, click on **Debug** at the top of the factory. It's the icon that looks like the following screenshot:

The pipeline will execute in a debug environment. Nothing will be copied for real, but just executed to ensure that everything works properly. If that's the case, as shown in the following screenshot, you will see the execution results:

If you click on the small glasses icon as highlighted in the previous screenshot, you will see more details about the activity execution, as shown here:

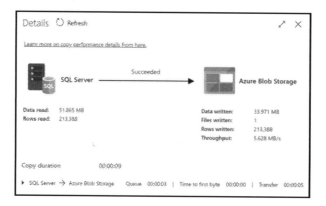

Publish and trigger the copy activity

We'll now publish the new pipeline to be able to execute the copy activity. Click on the **Publish** button at the top of the factory. Once everything is published, click on the **Trigger** button at the top of the pipeline. As shown in the following screenshot, select **Trigger Now** to execute the pipeline immediately:

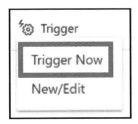

The **Pipeline Run** window appears. Since we do not have any parameters to set, we click on **Finish** to trigger the pipeline, as shown in this screenshot:

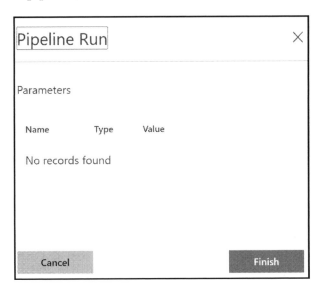

We'll now go to the monitoring section of the factory. As shown in the following screenshot, we can see that the `pipeline1` is executed successfully:

Now, we'll switch to the blob storage account and see that the data has been transferred. We now have a file called `Sales.txt` in our blob storage `sales-data` container:

 In real-world scenarios, the file would have used a scheme with the current date on which it was uploaded. When we have big data volumes, we use this date to partition our blob storage.

The last step is where we copy back the copy activity in the main pipeline along with the SSIS activity. Go back to the `pipeline1`, right-click on the copy activity, and choose **Copy** from the submenu.

Now, navigate to the `MainADFBook` pipeline and paste the content of the clipboard into it. Unfortunately, ADF will not keep the name of the activity at time of writing this book. We hope they will allow keeping the original name in the future. Rename it and attach it to the SSIS activity. Your pipeline should now look like the following screenshot:

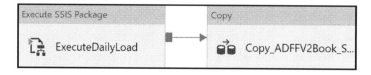

We now have data ready to be consumed by Databricks.

Databricks notebook

We are now ready to consume and transform data from the Sales.txt file we created in the previous section. We'll go back to the Databricks workspace and create a new notebook. The easiest way to achieve it is to use a template. As shown in the following screenshot, we select the **Data** icon in the toolbar at the left of our workspace. We go to **Tables | Spark Data Sources | Azure Blob Storage**. Click on **Create Table in Notebook** to create the new notebook:

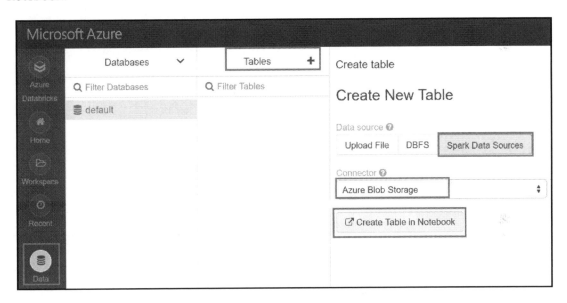

The notebook opens, with lots of sections. We'll first rename it, right-click on the notebook name and select **Rename.**

Enter ADFV2Notebook and click on **Rename** to rename it.

We'll now move it to the ADFCalls folder. Right-click again on the newly renamed notebook and select **Move** from the submenu, as shown next:

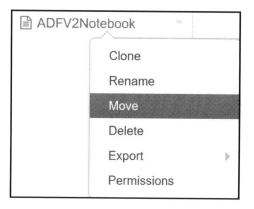

The following dialog box appears. Select the folder ADFCalls and click on **Select** to move the notebook to its desired location:

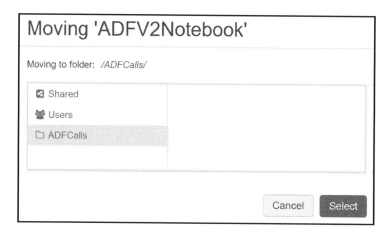

Now that the notebook is named and located properly, we'll modify its content.

A notebook is used by a data scientist to note how he/she conducted his/her experiments with the data he/she used. In our case, we'll do the following experiment:

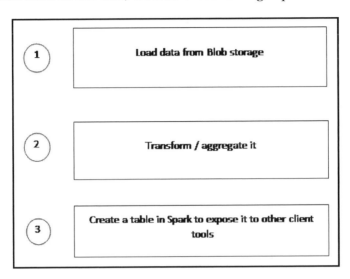

To execute all of the following steps in our notebook, we need computing capacity—a cluster. We'll make sure that the one we created earlier is running. At the top of the notebook, we have the status of the notebook, whether it is attached to the cluster or not. As shown in the following screenshot, we make sure the notebook is attached to our cluster:

To attach it to the cluster, click on the **Detached** icon and select your cluster in the list:

ADFV2Book (Terminated, 4.0 (includes Apache Spark 2.3.0, Scala 2.11))

Once attached to the cluster, we can start the cluster if it's not running, as shown in the following screenshot:

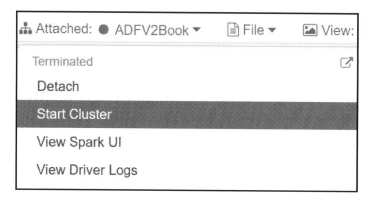

We are now ready to focus on our notebook. The first step will consist of indicating to Sparks where to find the source data and what format it is in. In our case, the source file is in our **ADFV2Book | sales-data** blob storage. At the top of the notebook, we have textboxes that can hold this information. This information will be used later by our ADF Databricks activity as parameters. The following list shows the properties that must be filled in:

- **Storage Key / SAS**: This is the storage key used by the `adfv2Book` storage account. It is accessible in the **Access keys** section of the `adfv2Book` storage account.
- **Storage Account Name**: This our storage account name, `adfv2book`.
- **Upload Location**: This property is a bit tricky to set. It consists of using `wasbs://` + the container name + `sales-data@adfv2book.blob.core.windows.net/`. In our case, we will use `wasbs://sales-data@adfv2book.blob.core.windows.net/`.
- **file_type**: CSV.

The textboxes are created by the first section of our notebook, as shown in the following screenshot:

```
Cmd 3
1   dbutils.widgets.text("storage_account_name", "STORAGE_ACCOUNT_NAME", "Storage Account Name")
2   dbutils.widgets.text("storage_account_access_key", "YOUR_ACCESS_KEY", "Storage Access Key / SAS")

Command took 9.98 seconds -- by ccots_1@msn.com at 5/21/2018, 9:14:38 AM on test

Cmd 4
1   dbutils.widgets.text("file_location", "wasbs://example/location", "Upload Location")
2   dbutils.widgets.dropdown("file_type", "csv", ["csv", 'parquet', 'json'])
```

The notebook described here has been modified to make it simpler.

The `dbutils.widgets.text` is declaring parameters that will be used later in the notebook. The next step sets the Sparks configuration, as shown in the following screenshot. We can execute each step by pressing *Ctrl + Enter* to test the steps one at a time:

```
Cmd 5
1   spark.conf.set(
2     "fs.azure.account.key."+dbutils.widgets.get("storage_account_name")+".blob.core.windows.net",
3     dbutils.widgets.get("storage_account_access_key"))

Command took 6.03 seconds -- by ccots_1@msn.com at 5/21/2018, 9:14:38 AM on test
```

This time, the command `dbutils.widgets.get` is used to read the parameters. We are now ready to go to step 3, reading the data. We'll use the following command:

```
df =
spark.read.format(dbutils.widgets.get("file_type")).option("inferSchema",
"true").load(dbutils.widgets.get("file_location"))
```

The df is a data frame, a structure in Sparks. It will hold the content of the container at `file_location` (`sales-data/`). The file is a `file_type` (CSV).

We can now create the tables. As shown in the following screenshot, the notebook is well-documented. We describe all the steps we accomplished in our notebook:

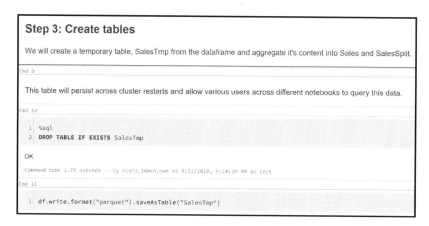

We first use `%sql` to tell Sparks that the next command will use the SQL language. Since we are creating a table from the data frame (which contains all files in our `sales-data` container—`Sales.txt`), we drop it first if it exists. If we don't do that, the next command will return an error. The `df.write.format...` command is writing the content of the data frame in a file on the cluster. This will become a table that can be consumed by later processes.

The last step creates a table that will aggregate the data of our file, as shown in the following screenshot:

The table `Sales` is the one that will be used in the Power BI chapter. To make sure that the notebook executes properly, click on the **Run All** button at the top of the notebook, as shown in the screenshot.

Now that we have a notebook, we'll execute it from ADF.

At the end of the notebook, we're making a query to observe the results. By default, the results are displayed in a grid. But one of the advantages of a notebook is that we can use some visuals to analyze the data inside the workbook. Clicking on the graph button allows us to see the data in some graphs. We can see an example of it in the next screenshot:

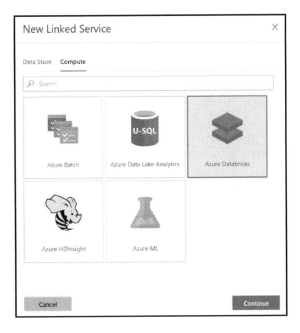

Calling Databricks notebook execution in ADF

We now have laid down everything to trigger the notebook execution in ADF. Going back to the factory, we're going to add a linked service. So far, all the linked services we created in this book were connected to a data store: SQL Server, blob storage, and so on. This time, we're going to use a computation linked service: Azure Databricks.

As shown in the following screenshot, add a linked service. Click on the **Compute** tab, select **Azure Databricks**, and click on **Continue**:

We'll now enter the details of the cluster in the next step. We used **Azure Databricks** for the **Type** property. The following screenshot shows the properties to set:

The properties are explained as follows:

- **Connect via integration runtime**: We use the **Default** one. It has access to all Azure resources.
- **Account selection method**: **From Azure subscription**.
- **Select cluster**: We're going to create a cluster on the fly and it will be running only for the duration of our job; therefore, we select the **New job cluster** option. It will be terminated later. If you selected the **Existing cluster** option, it would mean that you would use an interactive cluster, one that is already running outside ADF.
- **Domain/Region**: Choose the domain/region you have used since the beginning of the book.
- **Access token**: This one is a bit trickier. You can get it in your Databrick workspace by clicking on the user icon and selecting **User Settings** from the submenu:

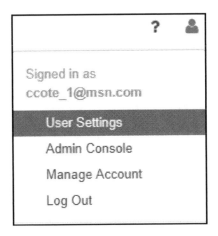

You are taken to the **Access Tokens** tab. Click on **Generate New Token,** as shown in the following screenshot:

A token appears in a new window. Copy it and store it someplace from where you can retrieve it later:

Going back to the factory, paste the token in the **Access token** textbox:

- **Cluster node type**: Choose the smallest node since you do not have a lot of data to process.
- **Cluster version**: Accept the default.
- **Workers**: This tells us how many machines will execute the work. Since we do not have a lot of data to process, we'll use 1.
- **Enable autoscaling**: We do not need to enable this in our case.

Click on **Finish** to complete the linked service creation.

We'll now add a new pipeline to our factory, and we'll drag and drop a Databrick's **Notebook** activity on it as shown in the following screenshot. Rename it `AzureDatabricks`:

Now, click on the **Settings** tab and adjust the properties as shown in this screenshot:

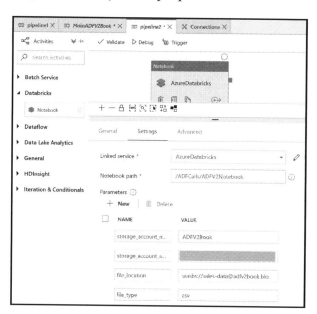

The properties are explained here:

- **Linked service**: Select `AzureDatabricks` from the list.
- **Notebook path**: `/ADFCalls/ADFV2Notebook`.
- **Parameters**: We click on **+ New** for each parameter we're going to add. They must match the parameter (widgets) system names in the notebook:
  - `storage_account_name`: ADFV2Book
  - `storage_account_key`: Your account storage access key
  - `file_location`: In our case, `wasbs://sales-data@adfv2book.blob.core.windows.net/`
  - `file_type`: csv

We can now click on **Debug** to test it and see whether everything works well. Once we do this, it will create a real execution in Azure Databricks. Going to the Azure Databricks workspace, click on the **Clusters** tab and you should see something like this:

Once the execution completes, we can see it in the list of **Job Clusters** with status **Terminated**, as shown in the following screenshot:

If we click on **job-11-run-1**, we can see the detailed run, as shown in the next screenshot:

Now, go back to the factory. Click on the refresh icon to refresh the status monitoring, as shown in the following screenshot:

We can now attach the `AzureDatabricks` notebook activity to the main pipeline. The final pipeline for this chapter should look like this:

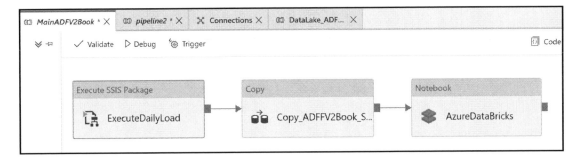

We can now delete the unnecessary pipelines used for development and publish all objects in the factory. Our factory is now executing an SSIS package that refreshes an on-premise data warehouse. Then it copies some data to the cloud to be modified further via Sparks Databricks.

ADF allows us to leverage hybrid ETL scenarios, both on-premise and in the cloud.

Summary

In this chapter we set up Databricks in Azure. We prepared and copied the data to be consumed by Databricks. Once done, we created a Databricks notebook. Later we used a computation linked service: Azure Databricks.

7
Reporting on the Modern Data Warehouse

There are a lot of tools available these days when it comes to reporting. In this book, we'll use Power BI for several reasons:

- It has a free version. We'll talk about the different versions later in this chapter.
- It can connect to a wide variety of data sources.
- There are many transformations and merges that can be applied to the data sources from it.
- It is easy to use and has a lot of visualizations available.

Power BI is not that new in the reporting world; it has been around for almost 5 years now. It has evolved since then and continues to evolve. Microsoft releases an update to Power BI monthly.

From a modern data warehouse perspective, we need a reporting tool that is flexible enough to accommodate a wide variety of users, from beginners or casual users to power users. As we will see later in this chapter, Power BI can address all of these mentioned users and can also connect to many data sources, be it on the cloud or on-premise.

The next sections will first explain what type of **BI** (short for **Business Intelligence**) a modern data warehouse solution should support. Later in this chapter, we'll use Power BI to create dashboards and reports on Azure Data Lake and Azure Databricks, as well as our on-premise data warehouse.

Different types of BI

In this section, we will discuss various types of BI depending on the use cases.

Self-service – personal

This is the type of BI or reports that users will work upon themselves. In this scenario, they use Power BI for desktop to connect to the data sources they want to, whether they are in the data warehouse or anywhere else on the cloud, such as Twitter feeds, data lakes, Spark, and so on.

Most of these sources require that users import data in the Power BI data model to their local machine. If the data source contains a large amount of data, this can consume a lot of resources. But in this mode, data can be altered, in the sense that the source data can be merged or transformed. No live connection is needed to connect to the data as it is imported to Power BI's underlying model. This model is meant to allow users to explore their data and modify it to suit their needs better. They have almost complete control over it.

If the data source is an SQL Server relational database or **SQL Server Analysis Services (SSAS)**, a direct connection can be established to it without importing the data to their local machine. In this mode, not much transformation can be done on the source data. This mode is meant to consume the data only. If it has to be altered, it should be done at the source via an ETL for a relational database connection or DAX in the cube.

Self-service BI is used at first as users might not know precisely what has to be done. Or they might have an ad hoc request and they need some freedom to analyze the data in a different way compared to the data warehouse.

Power BI for desktop is available via the Windows 10 store or at the following URL: `https://powerbi.microsoft.com/en-us/desktop/`. To do the exercises in this chapter, you must download and install this version. At the end of the installation process, you'll be asked to create or sign in with an existing a Power BI account. This account is needed to deploy the reports to Power BI on the cloud. If you don't have Power BI account, you can create one for free. We'll explain this in the section that covers Power BI service on the cloud.

Team BI – sharing personal BI data

Self-service BI works well if users only explore data and use it on their local PC. When they want to share their discoveries, they need a portal for it. This is where the Power BI service enters the scene. Users publish their Power BI models on the cloud and they can schedule data refresh if the data is available on the cloud. For imported data, there's a limit on the size of the model that can be published on the cloud. Currently, this limit is set to 1 gigabyte of compressed data. Power BI models try to compress the data by column to enhance query performance.

For on-premise data sources, data management gateways must be used. These gateways are like the self-hosted integration runtimes we used in previous chapters. They allow secure access to on-premise data from the cloud. We'll talk about data management later in this chapter.

There are two different versions of Power BI available on the cloud: personal and professional. The personal version allows publication of dashboards and reports to the cloud, but they cannot be shared. This can be seen as an extension of personal BI. We can show what we did but cannot share it. The professional version allows us to share our Power BI dashboard and reports with other users in our organization.

More information about the features of Power BI on the cloud can be found at this URL: `https://powerbi.microsoft.com/en-us/pricing/`.

Corporate BI

Corporate BI requires robust and performant solutions. There are two different scenarios that are used in corporate BI: on-premises or Premium on the cloud.

Power BI Premium

This version of Power BI is meant to be used by enterprises with many users and large volumes of data. It reserves resources on the cloud specific to the client. This means that we are assured to get lots of high performance when it comes to dashboard and report usage. This reserved capability comes at a price though, and there's a calculator that helps us define our needs that can be found at the following web page: `https://powerbi.microsoft.com/en-us/calculator/`.

For more in-depth information on Power BI Premium's capabilities, see the following URL: `http://download.microsoft.com/download/8/B/2/8B23B40C-E94B-49D6-AF19-456AC4D5DB00/Microsoft%20Power%20BI%20Premium%20Whitepaper%20Oct%202017.pdf`.

Power BI Report Server

This is an on-premise version of Power BI on the cloud. It allows us to publish Power BI dashboards and reports to an on-premise server to make them available enterprise-wide without having to bother about data management gateways for on-premise sources.

A license for Power BI Report Server is available with a Power BI Premium subscription or an SQL Server 2017 Enterprise Edition with Software Assurance. Once we have one of these, we can install it on a regular on-premise server and save our Power BI dashboards and reports on it.

With Power BI Report Server, we can also share SQL Server Reporting Services reports as well as Mobile reports. SQL Server Reporting Services is the reporting tool used to create corporate or official paginated reports. It's been used for more than a decade now. Mobile reports are meant to be used on mobile devices. They can show KPIs, graphs, and so on, and they are optimized for small screens.

Here is a link to get more information on reporting services and paginated reports: `https://docs.microsoft.com/en-us/sql/reporting-services/create-deploy-and-manage-mobile-and-paginated-reports?view=sql-server-2017`.

And finally, here is a link to get more information on Power BI Report Server: `https://powerbi.microsoft.com/en-us/report-server/`. For the development environment, there is a free version of Power BI Report Server available. Simply download the Power BI Report Server, and at installation time, choose Developer Edition in the drop-down list when you're asked to enter a license number.

Power BI consumption

So far in this chapter, we've talked about data publication. There are several ways to consume Power BI dashboards and reports:

- **Web browser**: This the most common way to consume the data when we are provided a valid URL for the reports.
- **Power BI mobile**: This is a client application (app) that is available for Windows 10, iOS, and Android. It has the capability to connect to Power BI on the cloud or on premises to a Power BI report Server. It is optimized for tablet and touchscreen usage.
- **Power BI embedded**: This allow us to integrate Power BI dashboards and reports in custom applications. They are mainly used by ISVs and developers to distribute their reports from inside their applications.

Having all of these possibilities to consume dashboards and reports gives us more flexibility when we design modern BI solutions.

Creating our Power BI reports

Now that we have explained what Power BI is, it is time to create our first reports with it. The Power BI development life cycle starts with Power BI for desktop. We create our reports with it and then publish them on the cloud or on-premise on our local Power BI Report Servers.

This chapter will focus on two paradigms of BI as explained in the previous sections: personal and team BI.

Reporting with on-premise data sources

Our first Power BI report will use the on-premise World Wide Importers we talked about earlier in this book. We will first connect to the World Wide Importers relational database using Power BI for desktop.

If you haven't created an account yet, create one now; it's free. If you already have a Power BI account, select the link as highlighted in the following screenshot:

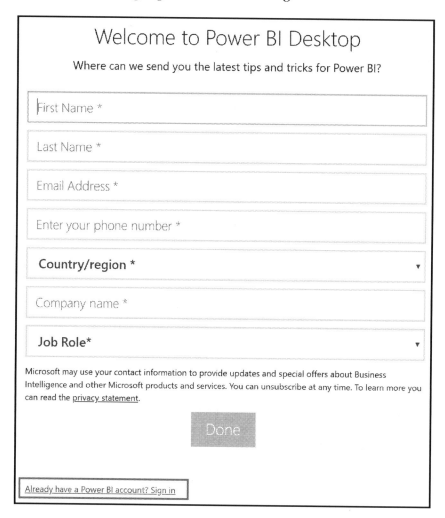

Once connected, uncheck **Show this screen on startup** and click on the **Get data**.

In the **Get Data** window, select **SQL Server database** and click on **Connect**:

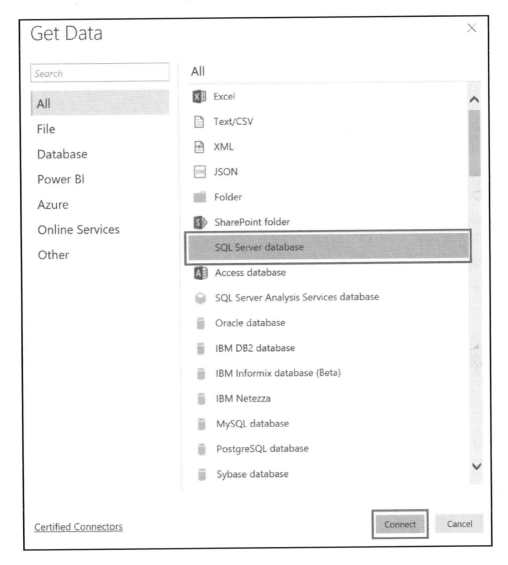

As shown in the following screenshot, enter the local on-premise server name and choose **DirectQuery** in the **Data Connectivity mode**. This mode doesn't import the data into the model; it only establishes a connection to our data warehouse database. This is the recommended mode to use when you are using a data warehouse as a data source. It allows access to live data and doesn't use space on the user's PC or in the Power BI service. Click on **OK** to proceed to the next step:

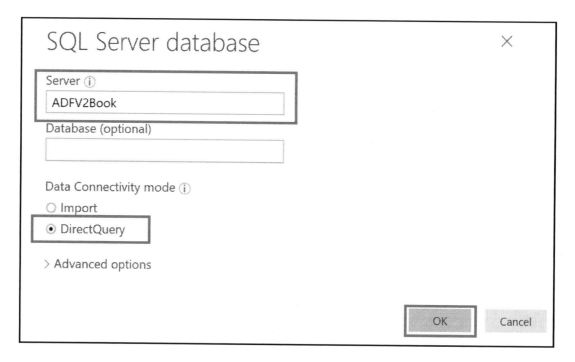

We're going to connect to the on-premise SQL Server instance where the `WWImportersDW` database is located. We'll use our current credentials for it. Select **Use my current credentials** and click on **Connect**:

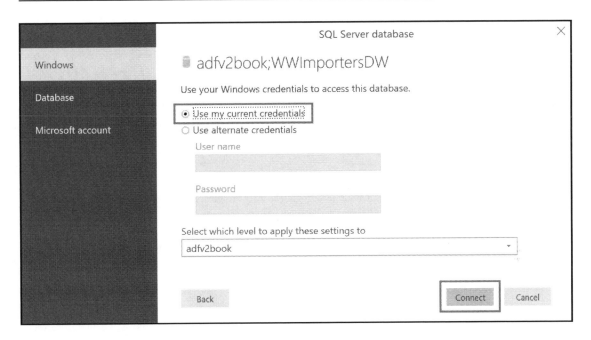

Click on **OK** if you see a message like the one in the following screenshot. It simply tells us that the data source we're using is not encrypted. In a real-world situation, we would like to have it encrypted to make it more secure. An SQL Server DBA would be securing the connection then.

The navigator appears; we select some dimensions:

- `Dimension.City`
- `Dimension.Customer`
- `Dimension.Date`
- `Dimension.StockItem`

We also select a fact table:

- `Fact.Orders`

Click on the **Load** button (when done) at the bottom-right corner of the navigator. You should get a screen showing you the connections created. Once done, you're back to the **Power BI Desktop**. As shown in the following screenshot, select the data view at the upper-left section of the Power BI for desktop window. The table you selected appears.

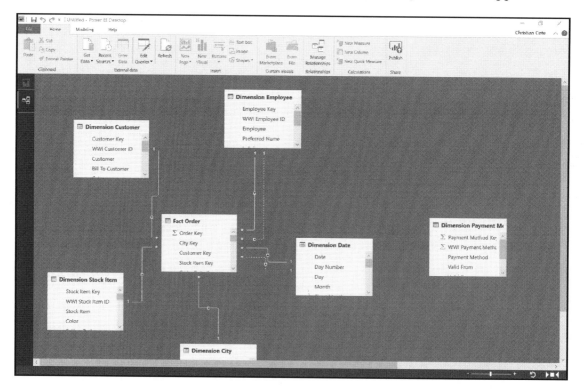

Data view for the selected table

Two dimensions, `Employee` and `Date`, have two relationships. They are role-playing dimensions. In Power BI, only one relationship can be active at a time. We're going to create two other dimensions. They won't be copies of the originals but rather pointers to them.

Select `Dimension.Date` in Power BI and click on **Edit Queries** in the top toolbar in the **External Data** group. The table definition appears.

Right-click on `Order.Date` and select **Reference** from the menu that appears:

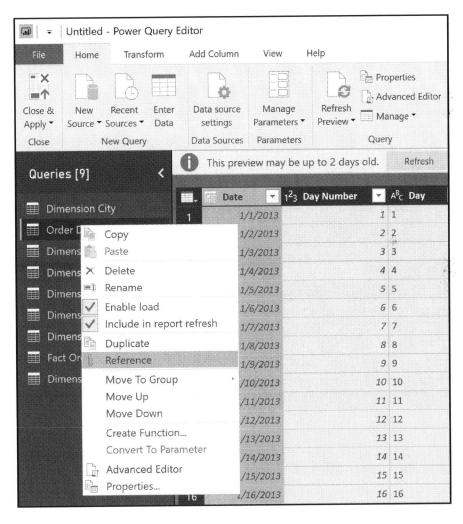

A new dimension appears in the **Queries** window: `Dimension.Order2`. As shown in the following screenshot, right-click on it to rename it as `Picked Date`:

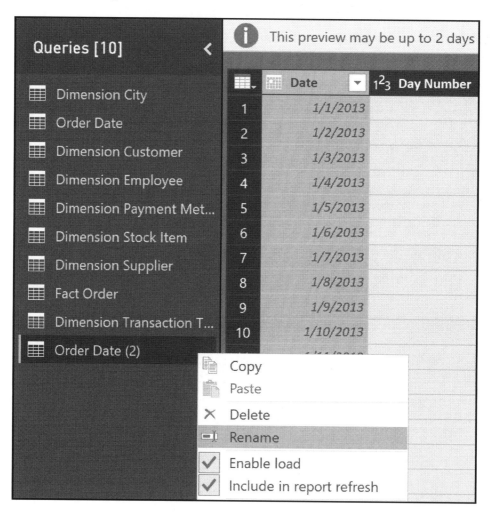

Click on the button **Close & Apply** in the toolbar to apply the changes.

Repeat the same exercise for the Employee dimension. Rename the referenced table as Picker and the original one as Sales Person. As you can see in the following screenshot, when a relationship is selected, the related columns are highlighted. As stated before, a table can only have one active relationship at a time. A solid line represents the active relationship and a dashed one represents an inactive relationship. Select the Picked Date table to delete the relationship. Right-click on the line to the Order Date Key in Fact Orders to delete it:

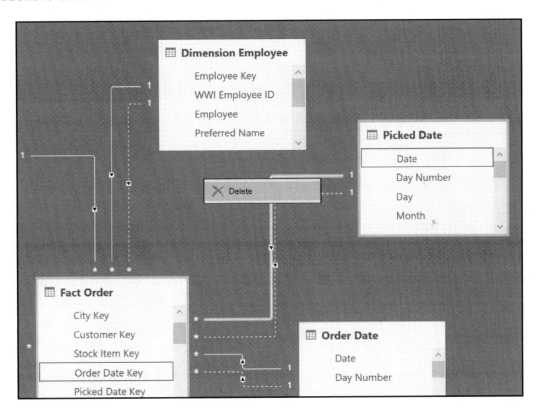

Now, double-click on the inactive relationship; the **Edit relationship** windows opens. As shown in the following screenshot, check the **Make this relationship active** checkbox at the bottom-left of the window and click on **OK** to complete the operation:

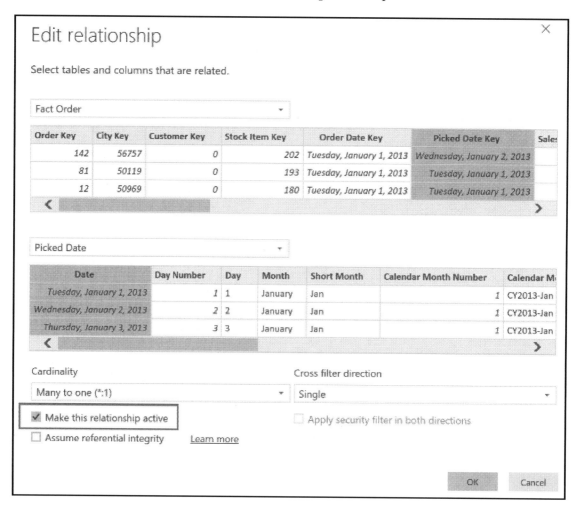

Repeat the same operation for `Order Date`, `Sales Person`, and `Picker` tables. Keep only one active relationship.

Now, we'll hide the surrogate keys and other unnecessary columns. To do that, we simply right-click on such a column and select **Hide in report view**, as shown here:

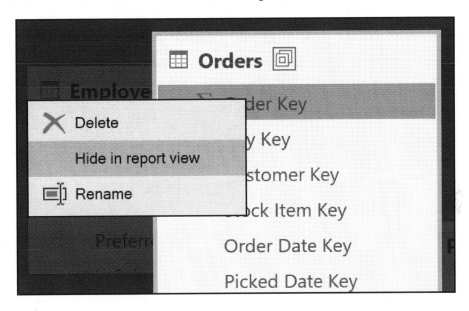

Your Power BI window should look like the following screenshot when completed:

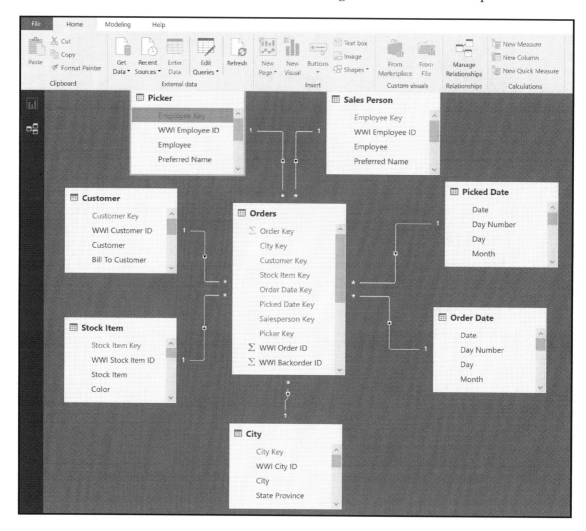

View after hiding unnecessary items

Now, let's go to the report view. As shown in this screenshot, click on the graph icon at the top-left of the Power BI window to switch to the report view:

You should see in the rightmost part of your screen something like the following screenshot—the **VISUALIZATIONS** and **FIELDS** panes:

We'll drag three visualizations on the screen: a slicer, a stacked bar chart, and a table. The final report will look like this:

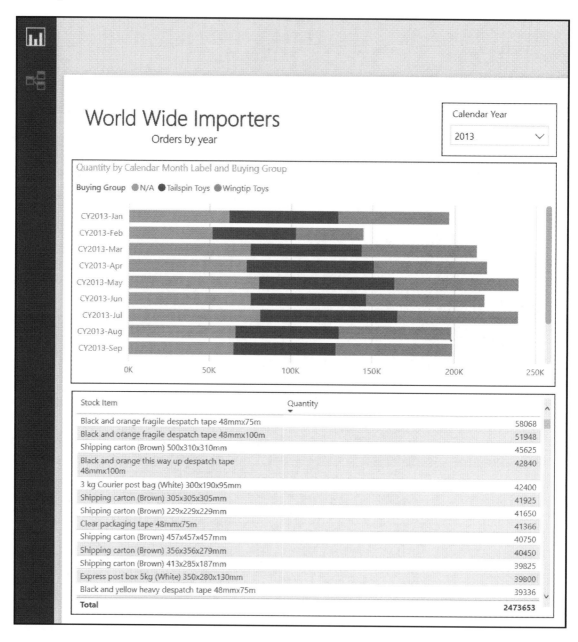

We first add a title to the report. From the insert section of the toolbar, select a textbox and drag it to the top-left of the report. Change the title to `World Wide Importers` and set the font to 28 pts. Press *Enter* on your keyboard to insert a new line and type `Orders by year`, as shown in the following screenshot. Set the font to 14 pts. Select the two lines, select the bold icon, and align them to the center of the textbox.

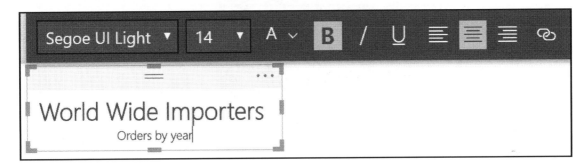

Next, we'll add a slicer for the years. Click on the slicer from the **VISUALIZATIONS** panel and drag it near the textbox you just added in the previous step. From the field list, drag the column `Calendar Year` in the `Order Date` dimension, as shown in the following screenshot:

Next, click on the roller brush and adjust the formatting parameter, as shown in this screenshot:

We'll now set the `Order Date.Calendar Month Label` sort property to make sure that months are sorted by month number (1-12) and not month name. If we don't do that, the visualizations using the calendar month field would show December as the first month of the year. Select the `Calendar Month Label` column and go to the modeling tab in the toolbar; click on **Sort by Column** and select `Calendar Month Number`.

This will make sure that the months will appear in a natural order from January to December. Now, we'll click on the stacked bar chart in the **VISUALIZATIONS** pane. We drag the `Calendar Month Label` and the `Date` fields from the `Order Date` dimension to the **Axis** property of the chart. We also drag the `Buying Group` field from the `Customer` dimension to the **Legend** property, and then the `Quantity` field from the `Fact Orders` fact table to the **Value** property, as shown in the following screenshot:

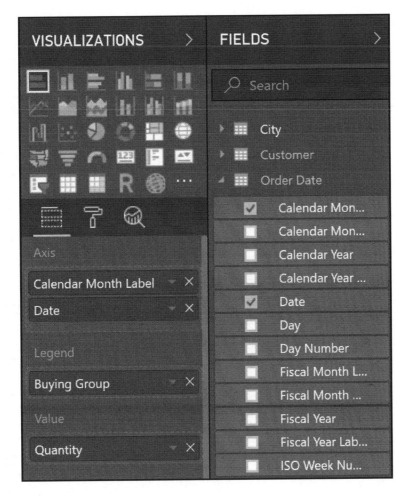

Finally, we'll add a table from the **VISUALIZATIONS** pane, and set the value using the fields Quantity from the Fact Orders and Stock Item from the dimension Stock Item.

For all the visualizations except the textbox, set the **Border** property in the format pane to **On**.

We have now finished our first Power BI report! Now, we'll publish it to the cloud. Click on **Publish** in the far right part of the toolbar. The **Publish to Power BI** window opens, as shown in the following screenshot. Leave the destination as `My workspace`, the default, and click on the **Select** button in the lower right of the window:

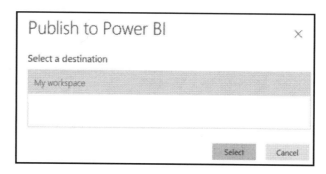

The report will be published to the Power BI service on the cloud. You may get a warning that the report cannot run since your data warehouse source is not available. This is normal since we're missing an important part of our deployment: the data gateway.

Click on **Open ADFBook.pbix in Power BI** as shown in the earlier screenshot to open the Power BI portal. Once in there, click on the Download icon at the top right and select **Data gateway**.

The **On-premises data gateway installer** opens once downloaded. As shown in the following screenshot, ensure that the **recommended** data gateway option is selected and click on **Next**:

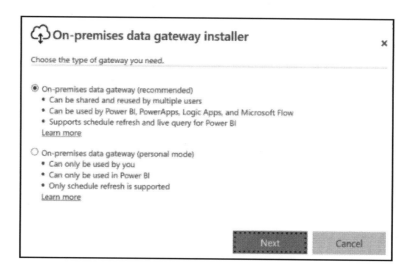

Enter a name and password for the recovery key and click on **Configure**, as shown in this screenshot:

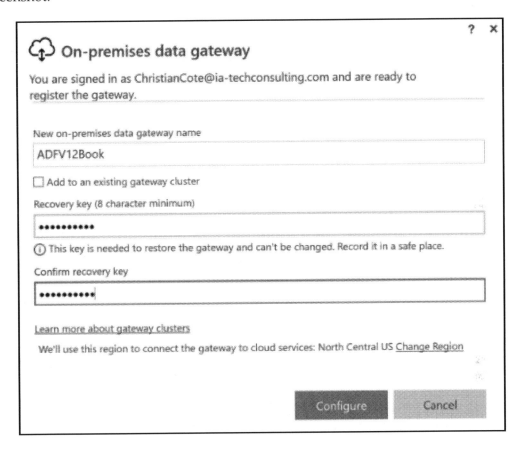

A screen like the following is displayed once the data gateway is configured. Click on **Close** to get rid of it:

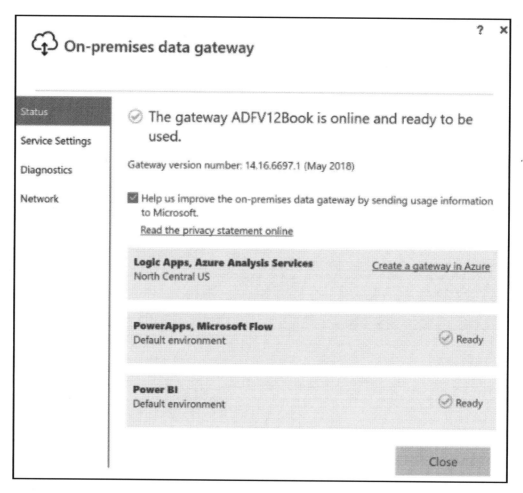

Having a data gateway configured is the first step. Now, we'll add a connection to our on-premise data warehouse to it. Click on the settings gear at the top right of the toolbar and select **Manage gateways** from the menu that appears.

Select `ADFV2Cookboox` data gateway and click on **New data source**. Set the data source settings as shown in the following screenshot. Set the **Authentication Method** to **Windows**; use your Windows username and password as the credentials. Once done, click on the **Add** button:

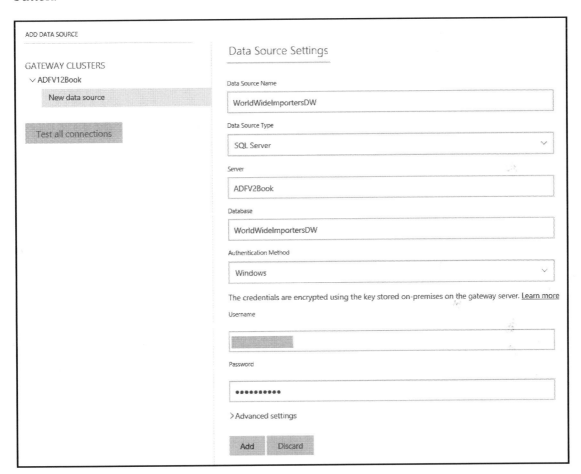

You should get to a screen like this:

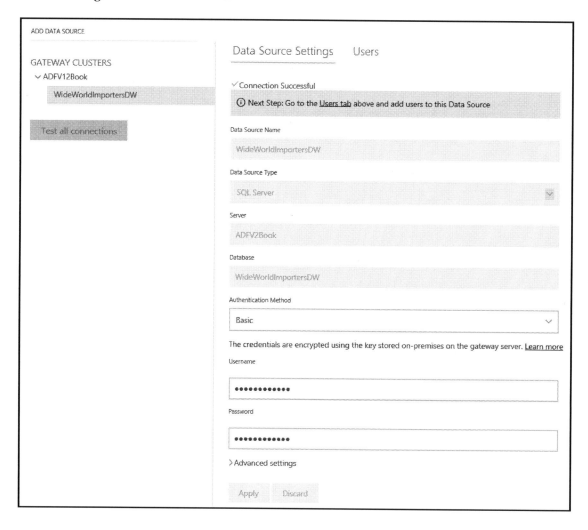

Power BI service can now connect to our on-premise data warehouse. We can now go back to the report and see that it works properly, as shown in the following screenshot:

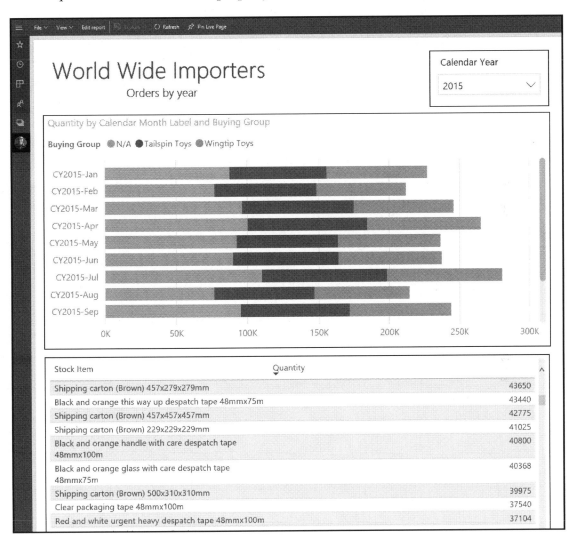

Incorporating Spark data

Now that we have created a report on the on-premise data warehouse, we'll add some data from the cloud to it. We'll add the table we created using Databricks. To extract data from there, the cluster must be an interactive one and must also be running. To connect to Spark from Power BI, we need to use a connector that is in preview but works quite well for now.

To connect to SQL Server on-premise, we used the direct query mode. Direct query is very convenient because it does not require importing the data into the model, but it has some limitations. The one that affects us the most is that we cannot use it when the model is connected to more than one database. We're going to connect the model to the Spark cluster, so we'll lose the direct query capability of SQL Server, but our Power BI model will contain data from multiple sources.

To connect to the Spark cluster, we'll use the JDBC connection available with the premium version of our Databricks cluster. As shown in the following screenshot, click on **Get Data** in the Power BI toolbar and select the **Spark (Beta)** connector:

We may receive a message saying that the connector is still under development. Click on **Continue** to dismiss that window.

The next screen will ask us to select the server and the protocol. We'll use HTTP for the protocol. For the server name, it's a bit tricky with this connector.

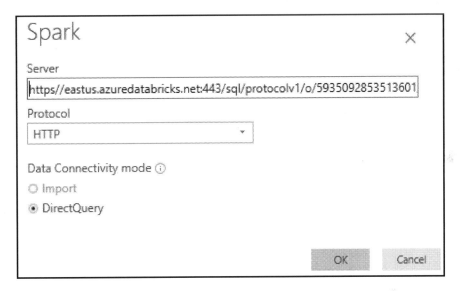

First, we go to the cluster in Databricks and, as shown in the following screenshot, click on **JDBC/ODBC**:

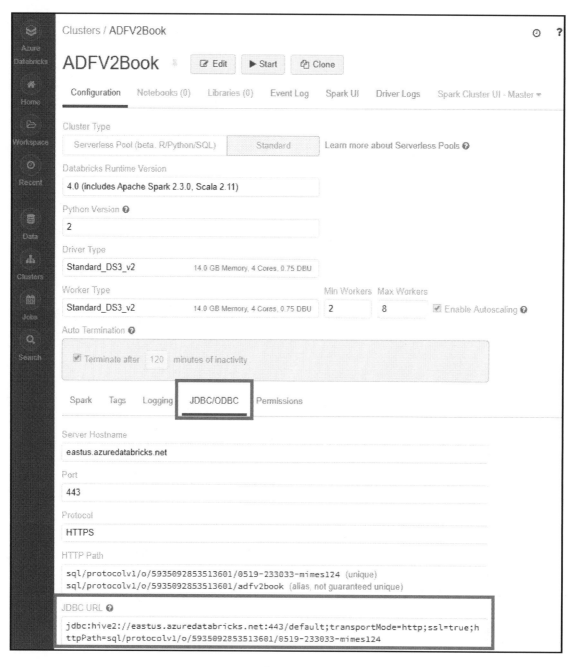

Now, the way to construct the server string is as follows—we replace `jdbc:hive2` with `https` and keep the substring up until `:443/`, as shown in the following screenshot:

Becomes `https://eastus.azuredatabricks.net:443/`. Then, we use the second part by using the last part of the string:

sql/protocolv1/o/5935092853513601/0519-233033-mimes124

So, the server becomes:
`https://eastus.azuredatabricks.net:443/sql/protocolv1/o/593509285351360 1/0519-233033-mimes124`.

Next, we use the same token as we used in ADF as our password and token as our username to complete the connection, as shown in the following screenshot:

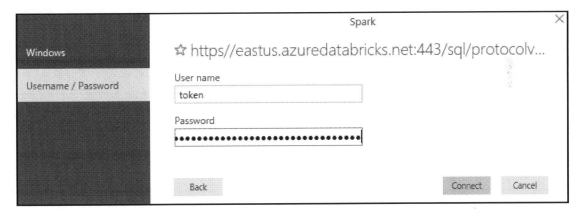

The navigator appears, and we can select the `sales` table. Click on **Load** to add the table to the model.

Now, this is where we face the limit of the Power BI direct query. As shown in the following screenshot, we're asked to switch to import mode. Click on **Switch** to proceed. The model will then import all tables' data, SQL Server, and Spark:

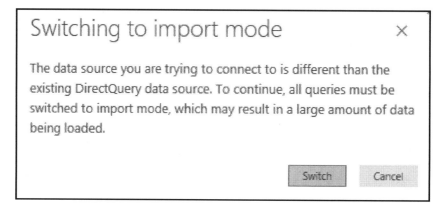

Switching to import mode   ×

The data source you are trying to connect to is different than the
existing DirectQuery data source. To continue, all queries must be
switched to import mode, which may result in a large amount of data
being loaded.

Switch   Cancel

Switch to relationships mode and link the `Order Date` dimension to the `Date` column of the `sales` table. Do the same for the `Customer` dimension, as shown in this screenshot:

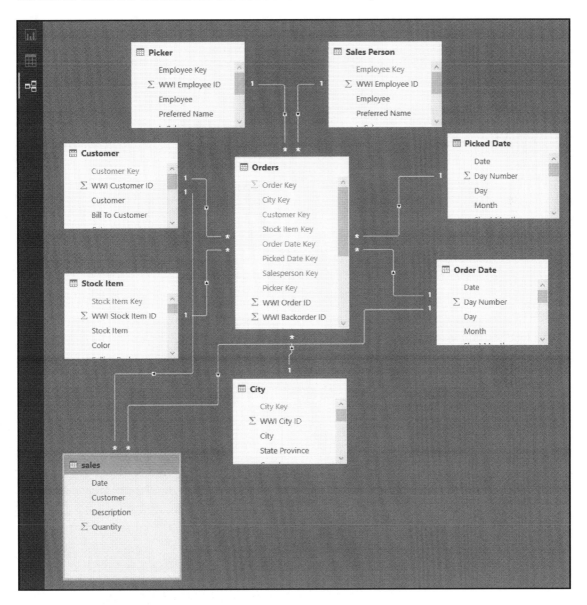

Now that we have linked the Spark table to the data warehouse tables, we go to the report view and add a new page to Power BI by clicking on the + sign at the bottom of the first page, as shown in the following screenshot:

We're now going to produce the following page:

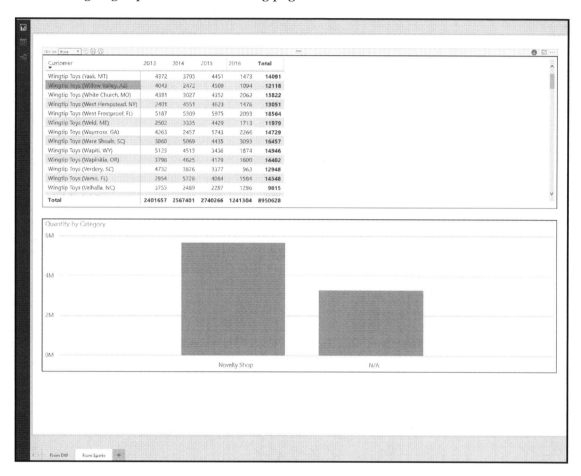

New page in report view

At the top of the page, we insert a matrix visualization and set its fields as shown in the following screenshot:

Rows:

- Customer
- Bill To Customer
- Primary Contact

Columns:

- Calendar Year
- Calendar Month Label
- Date

Values: Quantity

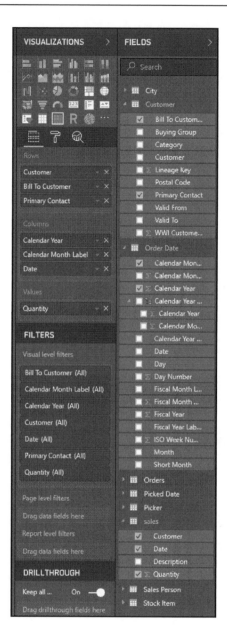

The lower visualization is a stacked column chart. Here is the fields usage of the chart:

- **Shared axis**: `Category`
- **Column values**: `Quantity`

And here is a screenshot of the fields usage:

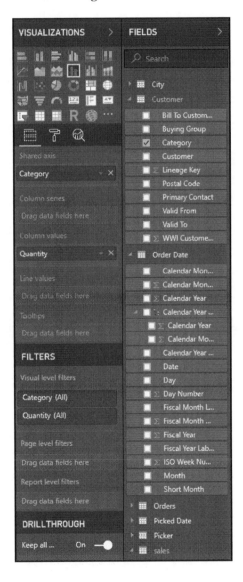

That's it! We now have a report based on both on-premise and cloud data. We'll publish it to the Power BI service on the cloud. As we did earlier in this chapter, we click on the **Publish** button in the Power BI toolbar. The following window appears:

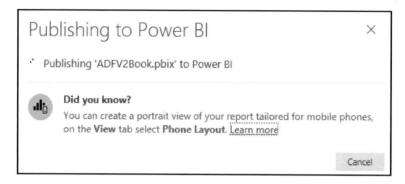

It might take some time as the data is also uploaded on the cloud. Once completed, the following window appears:

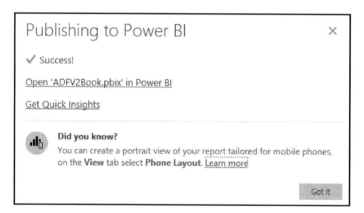

Click on **Open 'ADFV2Book.pbix' in Power BI** to go the report on the cloud, as shown in the following screenshot:

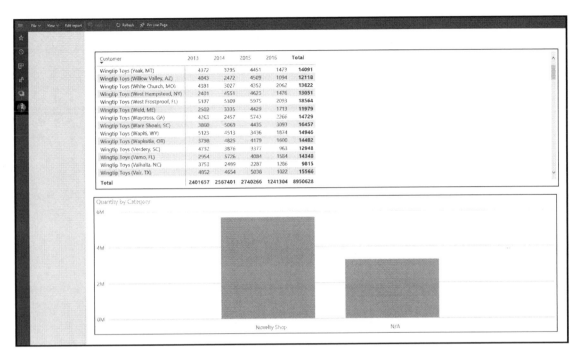

Report on the cloud

Summary

Power BI is a great tool to report on data warehouse and cloud data. This chapter showed how we can link data that is not necessarily part of a traditional data warehouse. As a recap from Chapter 1, *The Modern Data Warehouse*, a modern data warehouse is based on multiple data sources, both on-premise and cloud-based. ADF allows us to load all data necessary for a modern data warehouse, that is, from multiple data sources.

Index

C

classifier 159
cloud-based BI 8, 9
clustering methods
  used, for identifying groups 161, 162, 163
components, modern data warehouse
  consumption layer 12
  datasets 12
  linked services 12
  pipeline 12
  staging area 10
copy activity
  publishing 213, 214
  triggering 213, 214
corporate BI
  Power BI Report Server 232
  premium 231
  premium, reference 232

D

Data Explorer 104
Data Factory Pipeline
  U-SQL task, executing for data summarization
    133
Data Factory
  used, for copying/importing data from SQL Server
    to Blob Storage file 115, 122, 129, 133
data factory
  used, for data manipulation in Data Lake 115
Data Lake Analytics
  resource, creating 109, 112, 114
  U-SQL, executing from job 142, 147, 149
Data Lake Store
  configuring 99, 102
  creating 102
  data factory, used for data manipulation 115
  data, copying/ importing from database 103
  data, moving 103
  files, copying directly 104
  imported data, storing in files 103
  prerequisites 106
  reference 105
  service principal authentication 136, 141
  steps 103

Data Vault 2.0
  reference link 11
data warehouse
  cloud-based BI 8, 9
  IT driven 8
  need for 7
  self-service BI 8
data
  coping, from SQL Server to sales-data 211, 212
  preparing, for ingest 196
Databricks notebook execution
  calling, in ADF 221, 222, 224, 227
Databricks notebook
  creating 215, 217, 218, 220
datasets
  about 25
  integration runtimes 26
  linked services 25
  setup 206
decision support systems (DSS) 8
dimensionality reduction
  feature extraction 165, 166
  feature selection 164
  used, for improving performance 163

E

encryption Enabled option
  reference 100
experiment, Azure Machine Learning Studio
  datasets, loading 173
  module 173
  work area 174

F

feature selection
  about 164
  embedded class 164
  filter class 164
  wrapper class 164
features, ADF V2.0
  datasets 14
  expressions 16
  flow of activities, controlling 16
  integration runtime 14

89394767R00160

Made in the USA
San Bernardino, CA
24 September 2018